easy
Web Pages

See it done

Do it yourself

que®

Copyright© 1999 by Que® Corporation

International Standard Book Number: 0-7897-1796-4

Library of Congress Catalog Card Number: 98-86225

02 01 00 99   4 3 2 1

Interpretation of the printing code: the rightmost double-digit number is the year of the book's printing; the rightmost single-digit, the number of the book's printing. For example, a printing code of 99-1 shows that the first printing of the book occurred in 1999.

Composed in Baker Signet by Macmillan Computer Publishing

Printed in the United States of America

About the Author

Ned Snell has written 12 computer books and hundreds of articles and is the courseware critic for *Inside Technology Training* magazine. Between books, Snell works as a professional actor in regional theater, commercials, and industrial films. He lives with his wife and two sons in Florida.

Dedication

For my family

Acknowledgments

Thanks to the folks at Macmillan Computer Publishing—especially Scott Meyers, Mark Taber, Elizabeth Bruns, and Pat Kinyon.

Executive Editor
Mark Taber

Development Editor
Scott D. Meyers

Senior Editor
Elizabeth A. Bruns

Copy Editor
Patricia Kinyon

Indexer
Greg Pearson

Production Designer
Lisa England

Illustrator
Bruce Dean

Proofreader
Kim Cofer

Book Designer
Gary Adair

Cover Designer
Dan Armstrong

How to Use This Book

It's as Easy as 1-2-3

Each part of this book is made up of a series of short, instructional lessons, designed to help you understand basic information that you need to get the most out of your computer hardware and software.

 Click: Click the left mouse button once.

 Double-click: Click the left mouse button twice in rapid succession.

 Right-click: Click the right mouse button once.

 Pointer Arrow: Highlights an item on the screen you need to point to or focus on in the step or task.

 Selection: Highlights the area onscreen discussed in the step or task.

 Click & Type: Click once where indicated and begin typing to enter your text or data.

 Tips and Warnings give you a heads-up for any extra information you may need while working through the task.

2 Each task includes a series of quick, easy steps designed to guide you through the procedure.

How to Drag: Point to the starting place or object. Hold down the mouse button (right or left per instructions), move the mouse to the new location, then release the button.

1 Each step is fully illustrated to show you how it looks onscreen.

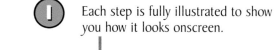

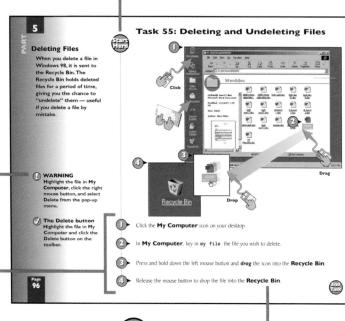

Task 55: Deleting and Undeleting Files

Deleting Files
When you delete a file in Windows 98, it is sent to the Recycle Bin. The Recycle Bin holds deleted files for a period of time, giving you the chance to "undelete" them — useful if you delete a file by mistake.

WARNING
Highlight the file in My Computer, click the right mouse button, and select Delete from the pop-up menu.

The Delete button
Highlight the file in My Computer and click the Delete button on the toolbar.

1 Click the **My Computer** icon on your desktop.

2 In **My Computer**, key in **my file** the file you wish to delete.

3 Press and hold down the left mouse button and *drag* the icon into the **Recycle Bin**.

4 Release the mouse button to drop the file into the **Recycle Bin**.

3 Items that you select or click in menus, dialog boxes, tabs, and windows are shown in **Bold**. Information you type is in a **special font**.

 Next Step: If you see this symbol, it means the task you're working on continues on the next page.

 End Task: Task is complete.

Introduction to Easy Web Pages

Anyone with a computer can write a Web page. It's easy—*really* easy, especially when you have the right tools.

The first tool you need is your PC and Windows (Windows 95, 98, or NT—makes no difference here), plus your Internet account—any Internet account will do. Those, and your imagination, is all you need to bring along. The rest of what you need you'll find right here.

In this book you'll find not only clear, simple steps for creating Web pages and making them look great, but also instructions for picking up a terrific, *free* Web page authoring program. The program and the steps work together to make you a fully functioning Web author—the *Easy* way.

PART 1

Getting Started

Most Web authors today—from beginners to pros—use a Web authoring program. A Web authoring program enables you to create a Web page in much the same way you would create a newsletter or flyer in a word processor. The better Web authoring programs—like the better word processors—are called *WYSIWYG* (what you see is what you get) because the program shows you what the Web page will look like online while you're working on it.

There are many popular WYSIWYG Web authoring programs. This book uses one of those programs, Microsoft's FrontPage Express, for three reasons: 1) It's free, 2) It's easy to get, and 3) It's an excellent program in which to learn about Web authoring. In this part of the book, you learn how to get FrontPage Express (or find out whether you already have it!), and get started in it.

But note that FrontPage Express has much in common with other WYSIWYG Web authoring programs, including its bigger brother, FrontPage. (FrontPage is Microsoft's pro-level program, not to be confused with FrontPage Express). The experience you gain here in FrontPage Express will come along with you, if and when you choose to move up to another program.

Tasks

Task 1: Do You Already *Have* an Authoring Program?

Start Here

There's a good chance you can skip Tasks 2, 3 and 4, and go right for the money. Why? Well, the Web authoring program used in most of this book—FrontPage Express—is a part of Microsoft's Internet Explorer 4. Internet Explorer 4 is included free on many PCs, so you may already have FrontPage Express. Here's how to find out:

✓ If you use Windows 98, you already have FrontPage Express—it's included with every copy. You can skip to Task 5.

✓ On some computers (especially new ones), Internet Explorer 4 has not yet been installed, but an icon for installing it appears on the desktop. This icon—sometimes labeled Set Up Internet Explorer—starts the installation procedure. If you don't have FrontPage Express, but do see this icon, skip ahead to Task 4.

Click

Click

Click

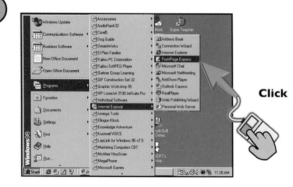

① Click the **Start** button.

② Click **Programs**.

③ Click **Internet Explorer**. If **FrontPage Express** appears on the Internet Explorer menu, you can skip ahead to Task 5. If not, see Task 2.

Task 2: Surfing to Microsoft's Web Site to Get an Authoring Program

 Open your Web browser (whatever you usually use to surf the Web is fine), and connect to the Internet.

 Go to Microsoft's Internet Explorer Web site at www.microsoft.com/ie/.

If you don't already have FrontPage Express, you can get it (free, of course) simply by installing Internet Explorer 4 and selecting the right options. You can get Internet Explorer 4 in lots of ways—for example, it's included free with many Microsoft programs. Get it any way you like. But in case you want to get it from the Internet, this task shows how to get started. (Tasks 3 and 4 show the rest.)

 On the Internet Explorer Web site, you'll find not only a link for getting Internet Explorer online, but also a link for ordering Internet Explorer on CD-ROM for a small fee ($6.95, at this writing). Internet Explorer is a very large program, so it may take a few hours to download from the Internet. You can watch TV, read, or clean house while it's downloading; still, if you don't like tying up your phone line, you may prefer to order it on CD-ROM.

 End Task

Task 3: Downloading the Setup Program

Getting Internet Explorer and FrontPage Express from the Web happens in two parts. The first is getting the setup program **ie4setup.exe**, as described here. The second is using that program to complete the download and setup, as described in Task 4.

Click

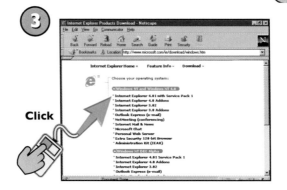

Click

Click

If you get Internet Explorer 4 in another way—on CD-ROM, for example—you must make one careful choice during installation to ensure that you install FrontPage Express. Early in the installation procedure (as described in Task 3), you'll be prompted to choose an "Installation Option." You must choose the "Full" installation option (not Standard, or Minimum) to include FrontPage Express in your Internet Explorer installation.

 Go to Microsoft's Internet Explorer Web site (www.microsoft.com/ie/) as described in Task 2.

 Click the link for downloading Internet Explorer 4.

 In the list for **Windows 95 and Windows NT 4.0**, click the version of Internet Explorer with the highest number (which will be the most up-to-date release).

 Click **Next**.

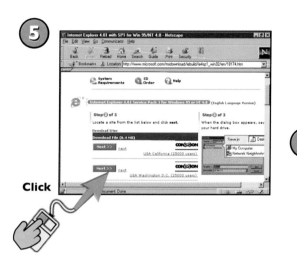

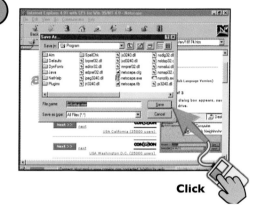

Click

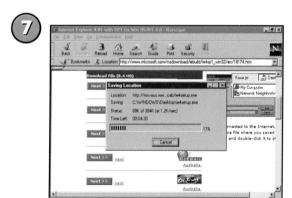

Click

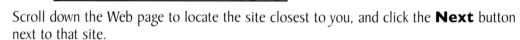

5 Scroll down the Web page to locate the site closest to you, and click the **Next** button next to that site.

6 Choose a folder (or your desktop) to save the Internet Explorer setup program in, and click **Save**.

7 Wait a few minutes while a setup program is copied to your PC. When the **Saving Location** box disappears, move ahead to Task 4.

In the example shown here, the latest release of Internet Explorer 4 is "Internet Explorer 4.01 with Service Pack 1." But new versions come out from time to time, and by the time you go to download, there may be an Internet Explorer version 5. That version may include an upgraded version of FrontPage Express.

The Internet Explorer setup program sets up Internet Explorer (and FrontPage Express) on your PC. If you downloaded the setup program (as in Task 3), the program automatically downloads the rest of Internet Explorer from the Web. If you got the setup program on CD-ROM, it automatically copies the Internet Explorer files from the CD-ROM.

Task 4: Installing Internet Explorer and FrontPage Express

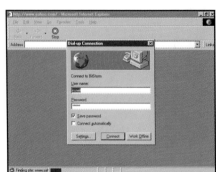

Double Click

Click

Click

Click

✓ Again, you do not have to use Internet Explorer for surfing the Web in order to use FrontPage Express. You can continue to use whatever you usually use for Web surfing, and use FrontPage Express for Web authoring jobs.

 Connect to the Internet (or insert the CD-ROM, if you have Internet Explorer 4 on CD-ROM).

 Locate the IE4 (Internet Explorer 4) **setup icon** on your desktop (or on the CD-ROM), and double-click it.

 Click **Next**.

 Click **I Accept the Agreement**, and then click **Next**.

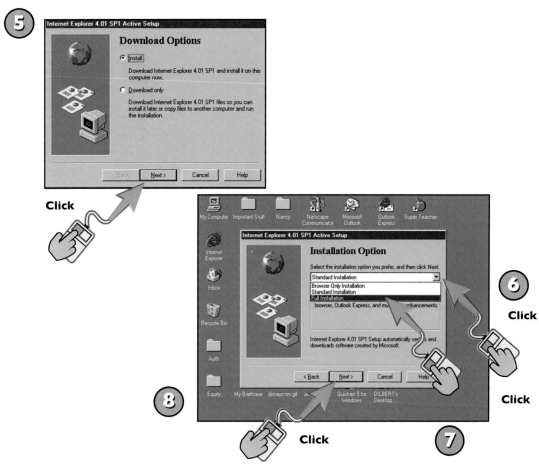

Click

Click

Click

Click

5 Click **Next**.

6 Click the **arrow** on the right end of the list box to open the list.

7 Choose **Full Installation**. (Only the Full installation of Internet Explorer 4 includes FrontPage Express.)

8 Click **Next**. Complete the installation by following the prompts.

When completing setup after step 8, you can pretty much choose any options presented, any way you like. As long as you choose Full Installation in step 7, you'll get FrontPage Express.

Task 5: Opening FrontPage Express

Once Internet Explorer has been installed (with its "Full" installation option, of course), you're ready to start creating Web pages. Here's how to get FrontPage Express open and ready for work.

✓ When FrontPage Express opens, it automatically opens a new, blank Web page file. You can start typing right away to begin creating your first Web page—although in Part 2, "Building Your First Web Page," you'll discover even easier ways to get a new page going.

✓ You close FrontPage Express by clicking **File** and choosing **Exit**, or by clicking the **X** button in the upper-right corner of the FrontPage Express window.

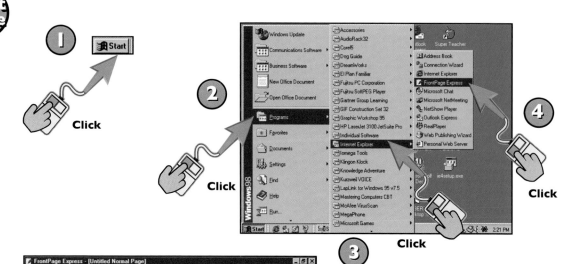

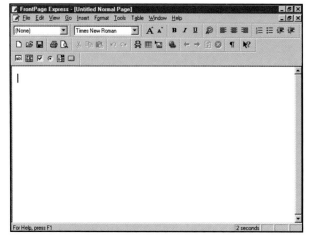

① Click the **Start** button.

② Click **Programs**.

③ Click **Internet Explorer**.

④ Click **FrontPage Express**.

Task 6: Discovering FrontPage Express's Toolbars

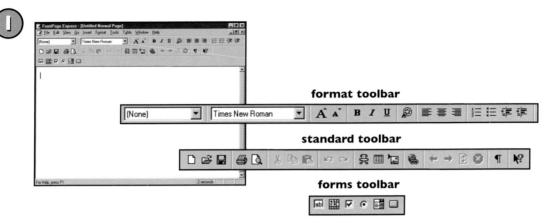

format toolbar

standard toolbar

forms toolbar

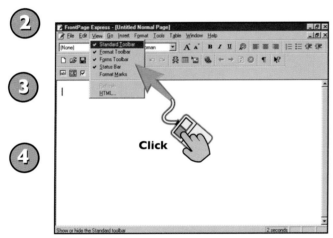

Click

You perform many activities in FrontPage Express by clicking buttons on its three toolbars: Format, Standard, and Forms. The toolbars appear as three rows of buttons near the top of the FrontPage Express window, and each can be displayed (for ready use) or hidden (to free up more screen area for examining your creations).

✓ Every button (or list box) on the toolbars has a "ToolTip," a name that appears to identify the button. To learn the name of any button or list box, point to it (don't click) and pause a moment.

✓ To quickly see the names of all the buttons in one toolbar (to help you locate a particular button), point to the button or list box that's farthest left until its ToolTip appears (don't click). Then slowly move the point to the right along the row. As you pass each button, its name appears.

① Open FrontPage Express, and look at the three rows of buttons beneath the menu bar.

② Click **View**. In the menu, a check mark appears next to the name of each toolbar that's currently displayed.

③ To hide a toolbar, click its name.

④ To redisplay a toolbar you've hidden, click **View** and click the toolbar's name again.

Building Your First Web Page

There's nothing more discouraging than staring at a blank page and knowing you have to find a way to fill it up. So when you create your first Web page, it really helps to have a head start, a basic pre-fab page you can change and expand to create your own.

That's what FrontPage Express's Personal Home Page Wizard provides: a head start. It doesn't give you a finished page all by itself; you still need to go in and personalize the page the Wizard produces. But you'll find that creating your first page is easier when you don't start out blank. The tasks in Part 2 show you how to use the wizard to crank out that first page in a flash.

Of course, you may soon want to create a new, blank Web page you can fill up with your own ideas from scratch. So by the end of this part, you'll know how to start one of those, too.

Tasks

Task 1: Starting the Personal Home Page Wizard

First things first: You begin your trip through the Personal Home Page Wizard by starting a new page in FrontPage Express.

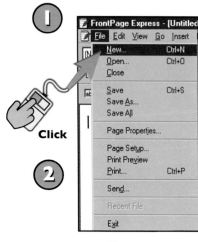

Click

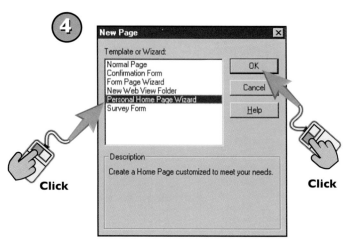

Click

Click

① Open FrontPage Express.

② Click **File**, and then select **New**.

③ Click **Personal Home Page Wizard**.

④ Click **OK**.

Task 2: Choosing What to Include on the Page

Start Here

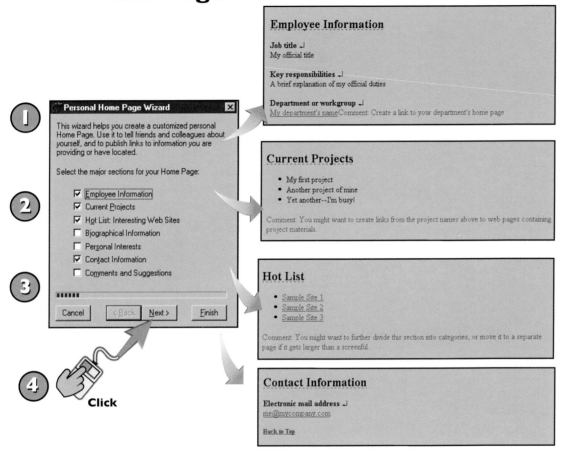

The Personal Home Page Wizard includes a family of different sections, each of which is designed to offer a different type of information on the page. In this part of the wizard, you get the chance to choose exactly which sections you want on your home page and which to leave out.

 Review the list of items, and decide which kinds of information you will want to include on your Web page.

 Change the check boxes so that check marks appear only next to items you want to include.

 For practice, leave check marks only next to **Employee Information**, **Current Projects**, **Hot List**, and **Contact Information**.

 Click **Next**.

 To add a check mark to an empty check box, point to the box and click. To remove a check mark from a check box, point to the box and click.

End Task

Task 3: Naming the Page and Its File

Like any computer file, a Web page file needs a filename. You should give your Web page files short, simple filenames, always ending in **.htm** or **.html** (your choice). All Web pages also have a title, which identifies and describes the page's contents to its visitors.

Personal Home Page Wizard ☒

The wizard needs to know what to call the new page. The Page URL is the name of the HTML file as it is stored in your web. The Page Title is what users see in a web browser. Most authors make their name part of the Home Page title.

Page URL

home.htm

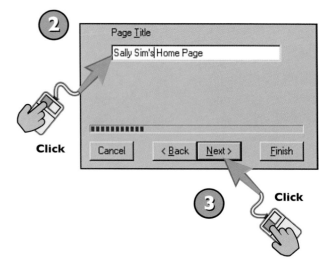

Page Title

Sally Sim's Home Page

Click

| Cancel | < Back | Next > | Finish |

Click

✓ At any point while working with the Wizard, you can click **Back** to go backward to earlier tasks and change your choices there. Your choices don't become final until you click **Finish**.

① Type a simple **Filename** for your Web page file. End the name with **.htm**.

② Click in the box beneath **Page Title**, and type a descriptive title for your page.

③ Click **Next**.

End Task

Task 4: Choosing the Information About You to Include

The Personal Home Page Wizard can include a variety of different sections listing information about you. You get to choose which sections to include and which to leave out.

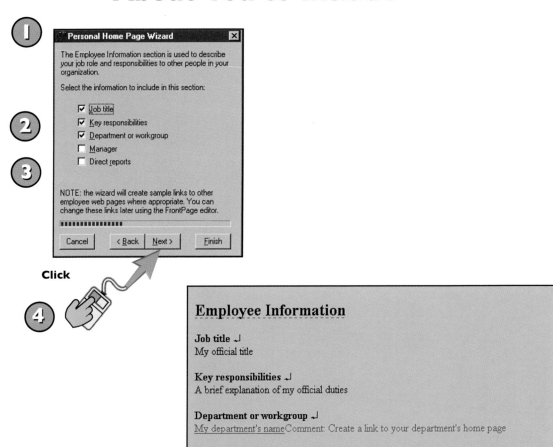

Personal Home Page Wizard

The Employee Information section is used to describe your job role and responsibilities to other people in your organization.

Select the information to include in this section:

☑ Job title
☑ Key responsibilities
☑ Department or workgroup
☐ Manager
☐ Direct reports

NOTE: the wizard will create sample links to other employee web pages where appropriate. You can change these links later using the FrontPage editor.

Cancel   < Back   Next >   Finish

Click

Employee Information

Job title ↵
My official title

Key responsibilities ↵
A brief explanation of my official duties

Department or workgroup ↵
My department's nameComment: Create a link to your department's home page

Comment: Change the sample links above to refer to the actual employee home pages, departmental web server, etc.

① Review the list of items, and decide which kinds of information you will want to include about yourself.

② Change the check boxes so that check marks appear only next to items you want to include.

③ For practice, leave check marks next to only **Job title**, **Department or workgroup**, and **Key responsibilities**.

④ Click **Next**.

✓ To add a check mark to an empty check box, point to the box and click. To remove a check mark from a check box, point to the box and click.

✓ When you're done with the Wizard, you can edit, expand, or enhance your page any way you like. So don't worry about making perfect choices at this point. Just take your best shot.

Page
17

Task 5: Describing Your Current Projects

The Wizard automatically builds a nice list of things you're up to. This is your chance to type that list. Of course, as with everything else, you can expand and edit the list later. But if you type it now, the Wizard takes care of giving it attractive list formatting.

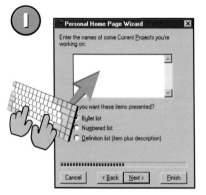

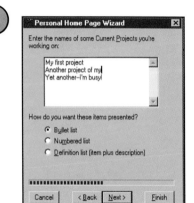

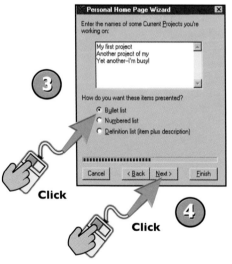

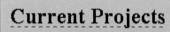

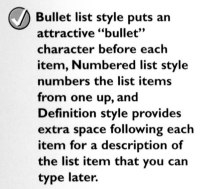

Bullet list style puts an attractive "bullet" character before each item, Numbered list style numbers the list items from one up, and Definition style provides extra space following each item for a description of the list item that you can type later.

Current Projects

- My first project
- Another project of mine
- Yet another--I'm busy!

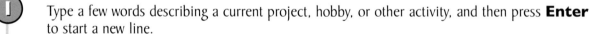

① Type a few words describing a current project, hobby, or other activity, and then press **Enter** to start a new line.

② Describe another project or hobby and press **Enter** again. Continue adding to the list, being sure to press **Enter** after each item.

③ Click the name of the style you want your list to be formatted as.

④ Click **Next**.

Task 6: Choosing the Style for Your List of Links

The Wizard whips up a snazzy list of links—a "Hot List"—so your visitors can jump straight from your page to other pages you'd like to share with them. Actually, the links are "dummy" links—ones that don't go anywhere—until you tell them where to go, as you learn to do in Part 4. The Wizard just helps you get started, like always.

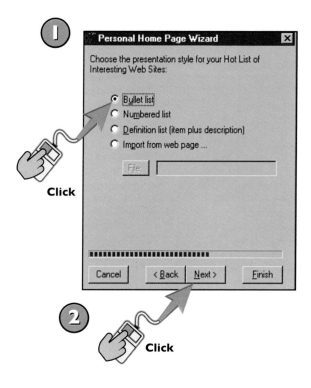

Click

Click

Hot List

- Sample Site 1
- Sample Site 2
- Sample Site 3

Hot List

1. Sample Site 1
2. Sample Site 2
3. Sample Site 3

1 Click the name of the style you will want the links in the Hot List formatted as.

2 Click **Next**.

✓ When you have more experience creating Web pages, you may choose the fourth item, **Import from Web Page**. This item copies a list of links from another page.

Task 7: Putting Contact Information at the Bottom of Your Page

Often, a Web page is intended to provide not one-way communication, but a two-way dialog. You have something to tell your visitors, but you also want to hear back from them, if for no other reason than to say if they like your Web page. That's where adding contact information comes in.

Start Here

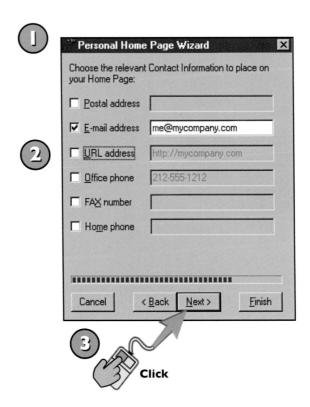

✅ To add a check mark to an empty check box, point to the box and click. To remove a check mark from a check box, point to the box and click.

✅ On a business Web page, it's often appropriate to include a postal address and a telephone number. But for privacy sake, never put your home phone number or mailing address on a Web page. Anyone who wants to contact you may do so by email.

1 Review the list of items, and decide which ways you will want visitors to contact you.

2 Change the check boxes so that check marks appear only next to items you want to include. For practice, leave a check mark only next to **E-mail address**.

3 Click **Next**.

Task 8: Choosing the Order of Information on Your Page

In Task 2, you decided which of the many available sections to include on your personal page. Now you get to choose the order in which those sections are presented.

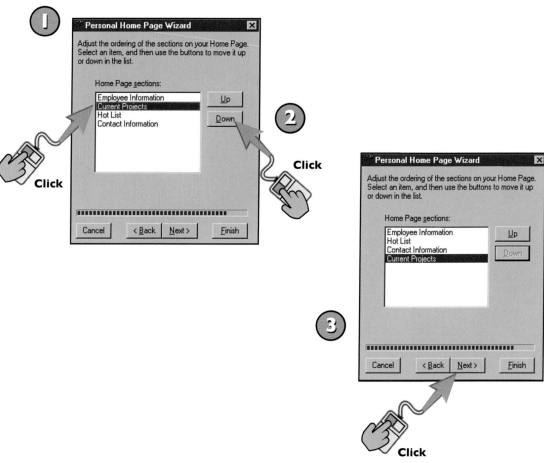

1. Click the name of a part of the page whose position you want to change.

2. To move the item higher on the page, click **Up**. To move the item lower on the page, click **Down**.

3. When the order appears the way you want it, click **Next**.

Task 9: Producing the Page

At last—the *coup de grace.* After having made all of your choices, it's time to tell the Wizard to make the page.

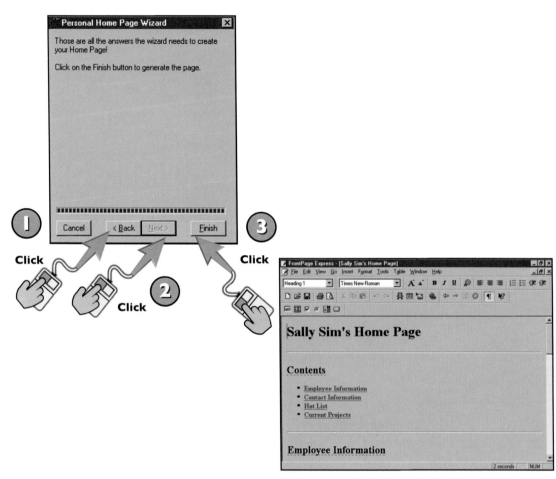

1. Click **Back** to review the choices you made in earlier tasks.

2. Make any changes you wish, and then click **Next** until you return to the final dialog box.

3. Click **Finish**. The page appears in FrontPage Express, ready for your edits, enhancements, and experiments.

Task 10: Saving the New Page

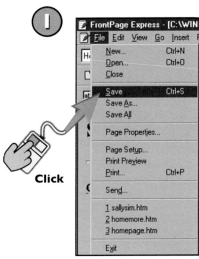

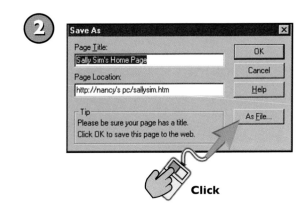

If you have any experience in other creative programs—such as word processors—you know how important it is to save your files. Web page files are no different. You should save your new Wizard-built Web page right after producing it, and then again anytime you make important changes to it.

✓ To save the Web page file in the **My Web Pages** folder you created in Part 1, do steps 1 and 2, and then find the box labeled **Save in** at the top of the Save As File dialog box. Click the little arrow at the right end of the box to drop down a list of choices. Find the **My Web Pages** folder in the list and click it. Then click **Save**.

✓ After the first time you save a file, you'll no longer need to perform steps 2 and 3 when you save again. Simply performing step 1 saves the file.

1 Click **File**, and then choose **Save**.

2 Click **As File**.

3 Choose a folder to save the page file in, and click **Save**.

Task 11: Closing and Re-Opening a Page File

As you work on Web pages, you'll probably create them over a series of editing sessions. You'll need to open existing files and close them when you're done.

Start Here

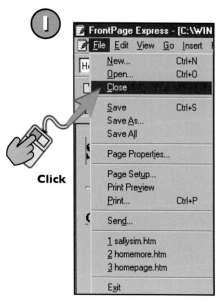

Click

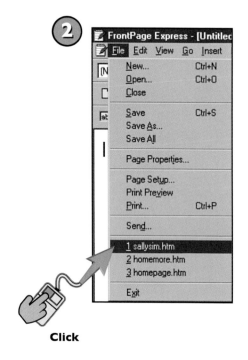

Click

① To close a page file (without closing FrontPage Express), click **File**, and then choose **Close**.

② To open one of the page files you've used recently, click **File**, and then choose the **page's filename** from the bottom of the File menu.

Task 12: Opening a Page File You Haven't Used Lately

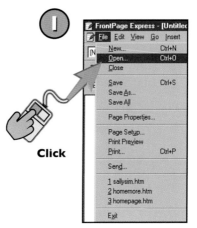

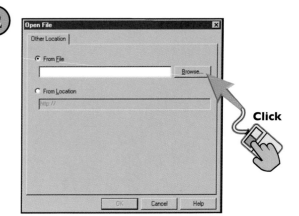

If a file you want to edit is not among the files you've edited most recently, its name won't appear on the File menu. **No problem—here's how to open any Web page file on your PC.**

Click

Click

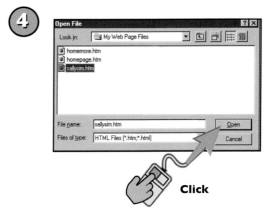

Click

1. Click **File**, and then choose **Open**.

2. Click **Browse**.

3. Use the **Look in** list to navigate to the folder where you stored the page file.

4. Choose the file's name from the **Open File** dialog box. Click **Open**.

Task 13: Changing Your Page's Title

The real "title" of your Web page does not appear within the layout of the page itself. It appears in the title bar of the browser through which the page is viewed, although Web authors often duplicate the title as a big bold heading at the top of the page layout. The title is important because it identifies your page in search tools like Yahoo! and in the bookmarks lists of visitors.

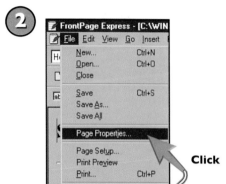

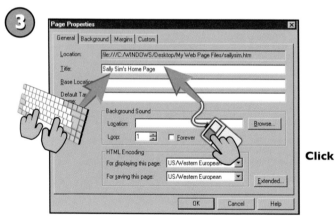

Click

Click

✓ Make your title short but clear and descriptive. In the example, it's clear that this is a personal home page for someone named Sally Sim. That's a much better title than simply "Sally's Home Page" because there are far fewer Sally Sims than Sallys.

1. Open your page in FrontPage Express.

2. Click **File**, and then choose **Page Properties**.

3. Click in the second box on the **General** tab and change the title however you want.

Task 14: Starting a Completely Blank Page

Start Here

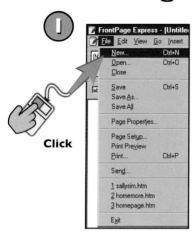

Click

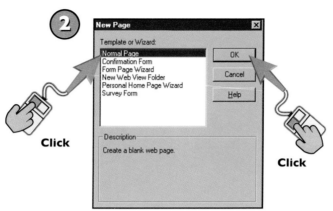

Click

Click

Now that you know the ropes of laying down a basic page with the Wizard, it's time to learn how to start a completely blank Web page you can fill in any way you want. It really doesn't matter which way you start—what matters is that you know about both methods, so you can choose the one you need on any given day.

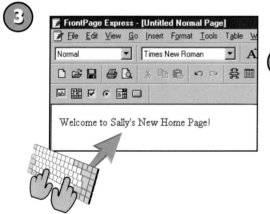

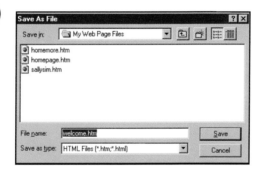

1. Click **File**, and then choose **New**.

2. Click **Normal Page**, and then click **OK**.

3. Start typing and formatting the contents of the page, as you learn to do in upcoming parts of this book.

4. Save your page early and often.

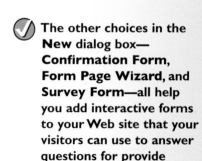

The other choices in the **New** dialog box—**Confirmation Form, Form Page Wizard,** and **Survey Form**—all help you add interactive forms to your Web site that your visitors can use to answer questions for provide feedback (see **Part 6**).

End Task

Task 15: Checking Out Your New Page in a Web Browser

In FrontPage Express, your Web pages will appear pretty much the same as they will when viewed through a browser and the Internet. Still, it's a good idea to preview your page through your Web browser from time to time to evaluate its appearance.

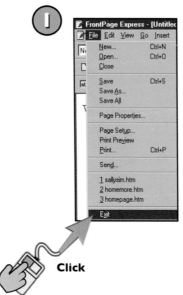

Click

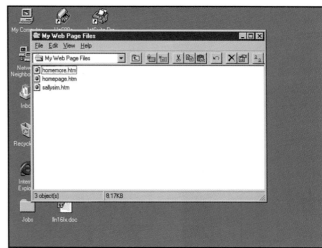

In Windows 98, you open a file icon simply by clicking it. In Windows 95— depending on how you have configured Internet Explorer—you may open icons by clicking or by double-clicking. If you use Windows 95, try clicking first, and if the page does not open, try double-clicking.

In FrontPage Express, click **File**, and then choose **Exit**.

In Windows, locate the file icon for your Web page file.

Double Click

③ Open the file icon by clicking or double-clicking it.

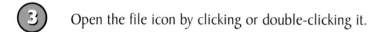

✅ Task 10 suggested saving your Web page files in the My Web Pages folder you created in Part 1, so you may find the file icon there.

✅ You may have several different Web browsers installed on your PC. But there is always one browser that's configured as your "default" browser. The default browser is the one that will always open automatically to show you a Web page file when you open that file's icon.

PART 3

Making Your Page Say What You Want

Pretty soon you'll start adding pictures to your page. And by all means, pictures are important. But it's the words, or *text*, that carry most of the content, that do the critical job of saying what you want your Web page to say.

In this Part, you explore the ways you create, edit, and format Web page text in a Web authoring program. You'll find that the job is very much like using a word processor—only easier.

Tasks

Task 1: Selecting Text

To perform most activities involving text—such as changing the style of text or replacing text with different text—you must first select, or highlight, the text on which you want to work. You select text in FrontPage Express in the same way you select text in most other programs.

Start Here

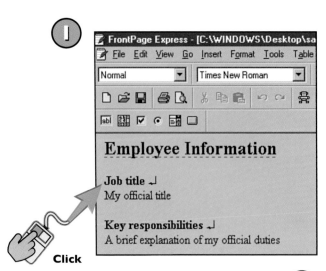

Click

There are two basic kinds of formatting: paragraph formatting (changing the appearance of whole paragraphs) and character formatting (changing the appearance only of selected characters). When applying character formatting, you must select precisely the characters you want to format. But when applying paragraph formatting, you need only select any part of the paragraph. Any paragraph formatting you apply affects the whole paragraph if any part of it is highlighted.

1 Click at the beginning of the text you want to select.

2 Hold down the mouse button **and drag** to highlight the selection: drag to the right to select all or part of a line; drag down to select multiple lines. When the desired area is selected, release the mouse button.

End Task

Task 2: Changing Text on a Page

Start Here

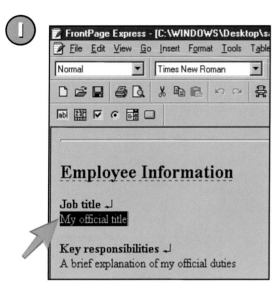

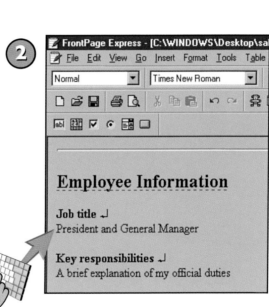

If you built your first Web page with the **Personal Home Page Wizard**, you've got a lot of sample text in your page that you need to replace with truly "personal" text of your own. Even if you don't use the Wizard, replacing text is an essential page-editing skill—and an easy one.

Select the text you want to change by using the click and drag method discussed in the last task.

Type your new text.

 Anything you type automatically replaces selected text. The new text is usually formatted the same way as the text it replaced.

End Task

Task 3: Typing New Text

Got a hole that needs filling with your thoughts? Just type away!

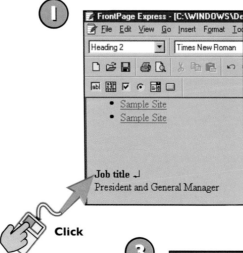

Click

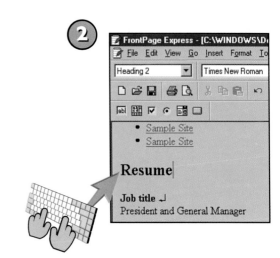

(✓) The edit cursor, a flashing vertical bar, appears where you clicked. Whatever you type appears at the spot marked by the edit cursor.

(✓) Don't forget to save your Web page file often, especially after any time you add or change text.

① Point to the spot on the page where you want to add new text and click.

② Type your text. When you reach the end of a line, just keep typing; the edit cursor jumps automatically to the beginning of the next line.

③ Press **Enter** to end a paragraph and start a new one.

Task 4: Typing Symbols and Special Characters

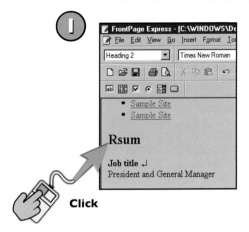

Click

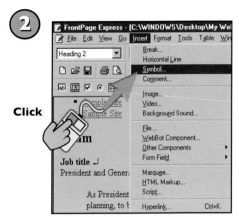

Click

Sometimes, you'll need characters that don't appear on your keyboard, such as the copyright symbol or the accented characters used in languages other than English. For such occasions, FrontPage Express offers its Symbol menu.

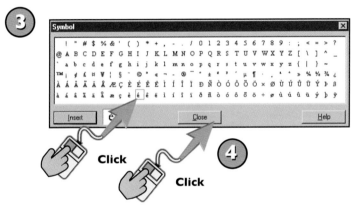

Click

Click

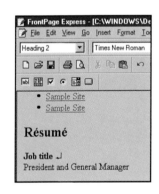

① Point to the spot in the text where you want to insert the character, and click to position the edit cursor there.

② Click **Insert**, and then choose **Symbol**.

③ Click the symbol you want to insert. After you click it, it appears next to the **Insert** button.

④ Click **Insert** to insert the character. Click **Close**.

 If you change the font of text containing symbols (as you learn to do in Task 14), recheck the symbols carefully and redo them if necessary. Sometimes changing fonts messes up symbols.

Task 5: Deleting Text

Wrote it, but hate it? You
don't have to live with it.
Wipe it out, and start clean.

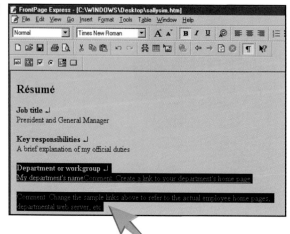

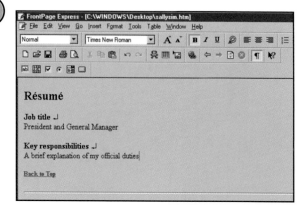

 Select the text you want to delete.

 Press the **Delete** key.

Task 6: Fixing Mistakes

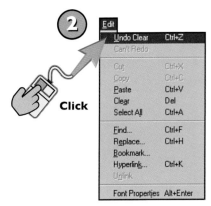

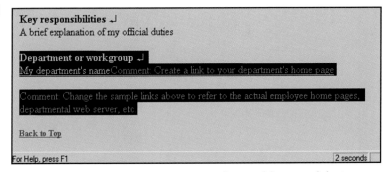

What better time to learn how to undo a mistake than right after learning to delete text? If you delete text and then suddenly realize that you want it back, you can use these steps to retrieve it. But note that these steps can undo almost any action you do in FrontPage Express. The catch is that you must use these steps immediately after the mistake; if you perform another action in the meantime, you'll undo that action instead of undoing the earlier mistake.

 The name of that top item in the Edit menu is always "Undo" followed by a description of the last thing you did. If you deleted, or *cleared*, some text in step 1, the top item on the Edit menu will read **Undo Clear**.

 You can reverse mistakes by closing a file without saving it (click **File**, and then choose **Close**).

 Perform any action in FrontPage Express, such as adding or deleting some text.

 Click **Edit**, and then choose the top item in the **Edit** menu.

 If you change your mind again, and want to undo the undo (putting the page back the way it was right after step 1), click **Edit** and then choose **Redo**.

Task 7: Copying Text

If you have a block of text you want to use in more than one place on your page, you needn't type it over and over and over. You can simply type it once, and then copy it wherever you need it.

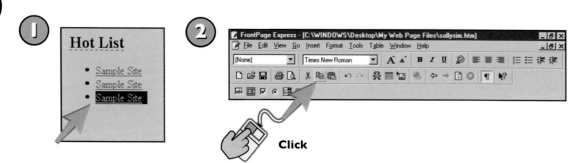

Click

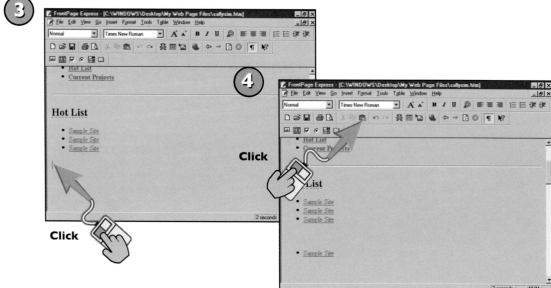

Click

Click

Click

After step 4, you can move ahead to other editing activities, or you can copy the same text you selected in step 1 again—and as many more times as you want—by repeating steps 3 and 4 for each copy you want to make.

1 Select the text you want to copy.

2 Click the **Copy** button on the Standard toolbar.

3 Point to the spot where you want to copy the text and click to position the edit cursor there.

4 Click the **Paste** button on the Standard toolbar.

Task 8: Moving Text

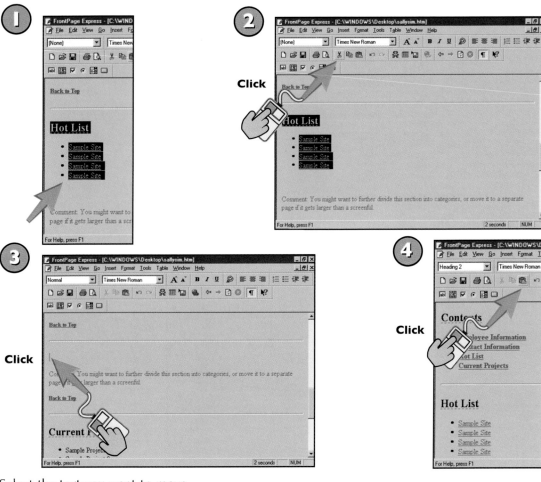

Click

Click

Click

Moving text is really just like copying—except that you don't leave the original text behind. You cut it from one place, and then copy it in another.

1. Select the text you want to move.

2. Click the **Cut** button on the Standard toolbar.

3. Point to the spot where you want to move the text, and click to position the edit cursor there.

4. Click the **Paste** button on the Standard toolbar.

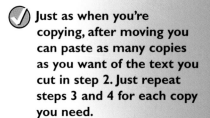 Just as when you're copying, after moving you can paste as many copies as you want of the text you cut in step 2. Just repeat steps 3 and 4 for each copy you need.

Task 9: Choosing the Style of a Paragraph

Start Here

The most important part of controlling text appearance is choosing its paragraph style from the **Change Style** list. The most important styes are the six different **Heading** styles (1 is the largest, 6 is the smallest), **Normal** style (used for ordinary paragraphs), and the **List** styles.

✓ Paragraph styles are an example of paragraph formatting (not character formatting), so you need not actually highlight the whole paragraph. Select any part of the paragraph; the style you choose will be applied to the whole paragraph.

✓ To apply a style to multiple, consecutive paragraphs all at once, click anywhere in the first paragraph, and drag down through the paragraphs to anywhere in the last paragraph, so that the highlighting touches all or part of all the paragraphs. Then choose your style.

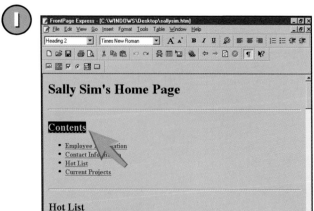

Click

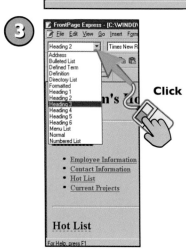

Click

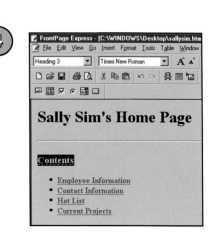

1. Select the paragraph whose style you want to change.

2. Locate the **Change Style** list box at the left end of the Formatting toolbar. (Notice that it shows the style currently applied to the selected paragraph.)

3. Click the **arrow** on the right side of the list box to open the list.

4. Click the name of the style you want to apply.

End Task

Task 10: Indenting a Paragraph

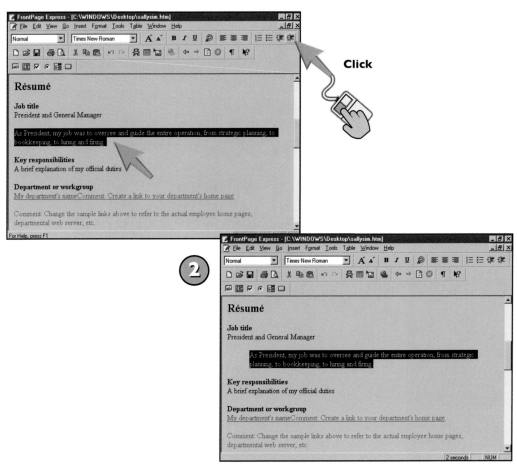

Click

To indent is to push text inward from the margin to make it stand out on the page and to better show that the indented text is a part of the heading or other text above it. Indenting selected paragraphs can give your Web page structure and visual variety.

Select the paragraph or paragraphs you want to indent.

Click the **Increase Indent** button on the Formatting toolbar.

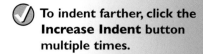
To indent farther, click the **Increase Indent** button multiple times.

To remove the indent, click the **Decrease Indent** button on the Formatting toolbar.

Task 11: Lining Up Paragraphs on the Left, Right, or in the Center

You can *align* any paragraph any of three different ways: tight up against the left side of the page (left alignment), centered on the page (center alignment), or hard up to the ride side (right alignment).

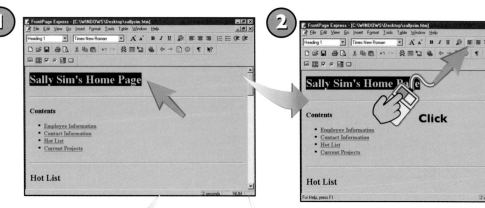

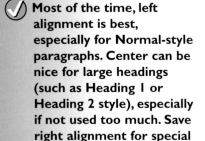 Most of the time, left alignment is best, especially for Normal-style paragraphs. Center can be nice for large headings (such as Heading 1 or Heading 2 style), especially if not used too much. Save right alignment for special needs.

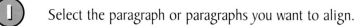 Select the paragraph or paragraphs you want to align.

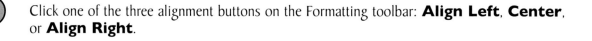 Click one of the three alignment buttons on the Formatting toolbar: **Align Left**, **Center**, or **Align Right**.

Task 12: Creating Lists

Start Here

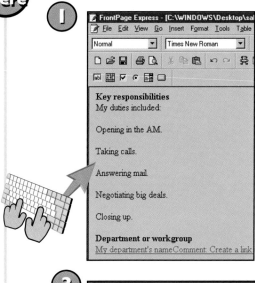

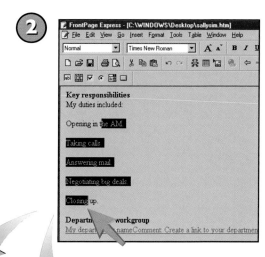

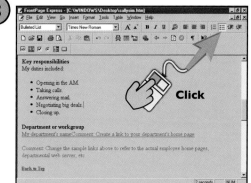

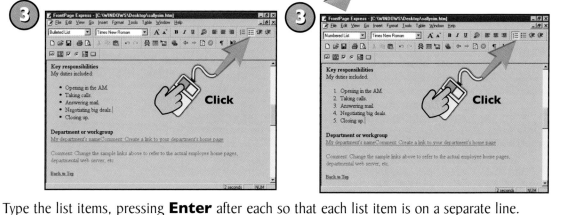

Lists come in two types. In a *numbered list*, the items in the list are preceded by consecutive numbers. In a *bulleted list*, each item in the list is preceded by a symbol—a "bullet" character—to give the list a little oomph. Lists are a great way to organize content while at the same time giving your page extra style.

(1) Type the list items, pressing **Enter** after each so that each list item is on a separate line.

(2) Select the entire list.

(3) Click one of the two list buttons on the Formatting toolbar: **Numbered List** or **Bulleted List**.

✓ List formatting is paragraph formatting, so you can select a list by starting the selection anywhere in the first item, and then dragging down to anywhere in the last item.

✓ When the order of the items in the list is important, as in step-by-step instructions, use a numbered list. When the order doesn't matter, use a bulleted list.

End Task

You can make a pretty good-looking list just by clicking a button, as you did in the previous task. But you don't have to settle for what you get. You can easily modify the appearance of a list, choosing the numbering style (A, B, C; I, II, III, and so on) or bullet symbol.

Task 13: Choosing (or Changing) the Style of a List

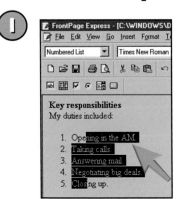

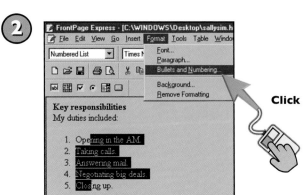

Click

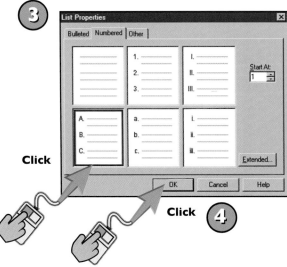

Click

Click

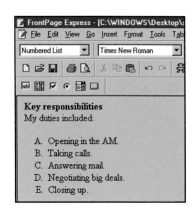

① Select the list.

② Click **Format**, and then choose **Bullets and Numbering**.

③ Click the new style you want to use from the options shown.

④ Click **OK**.

Task 14: Choosing a Font for Text

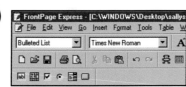

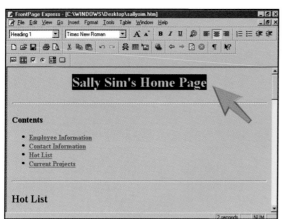

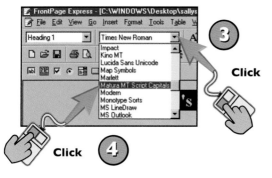

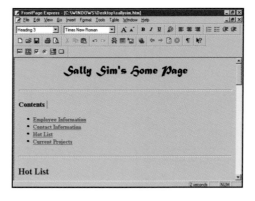

Click

Click

The best way to control the style of text is to choose the appropriate paragraph style, as you did in Task 9. But beyond the styles, you can dress up text even more by choosing a font for it from among those on your PC.

Fonts are a form of character formatting, not paragraph formatting, so they affect only the exact characters you select. To apply a font to a whole paragraph, you must select the whole paragraph. The same is true of the character formatting you discover in Task 15, "Making Text Bigger or Smaller," Task 16, "Making Text Bold, Italic, or Underlined," and Task 17, "Choosing the Color of Text."

Some browsers don't support fonts. If you've used fonts, visitors using those browsers still see your text, but they won't see it styled the way you intend.

Select the exact characters to which you want to apply a new font.

Locate the **Change Font** list box in the Formatting toolbar. Notice that the box tells the name of the current font for the selected text.

Click the arrow on the right side of the list box to open the list.

Click the name of the font you want to apply.

Task 15: Making Text Bigger or Smaller

The paragraph style determines size. For example, if text set in Heading 3 style looks too small to you, the best solution is to change it to a bigger style, such as Heading 2 or Heading 1. Still, you can fine-tune the size of selected text easily when the size chosen by the style isn't exactly what you want.

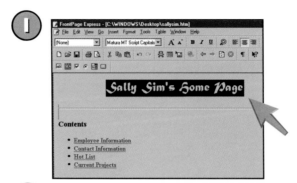

✓ You can click the Increase Text Size or Decrease Text Size buttons multiple times to make text a lot bigger or smaller. For example, to make text two levels bigger, click the **Increase Text Size** button twice.

✓ If you click **Increase Text Size** and the selected text does not get any bigger, the text is already set at the largest size allowed. Similarly, if **Decrease Text Size** does nothing, the text is already set at the minimum size allowed.

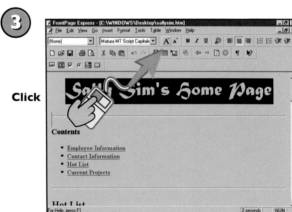

Click

1 Select the exact characters you want to make bigger or smaller.

2 Locate the two buttons to the right of the **Change Font** list on the Formatting toolbar.

3 To make the selected text larger, click the **Increase Text Size** button. To make the selected text smaller, click the **Decrease Text Size** button.

Task 16: Making Text Bold, Italic, or Underlined

Start Here

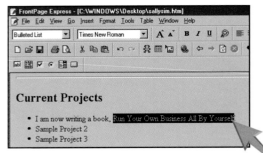

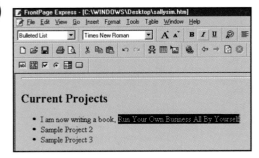

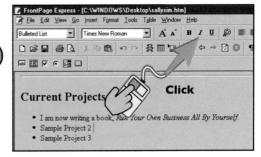

Just as in any letter or report you might create, **bold**, *italic*, and <u>underlining</u> are valuable tools in a Web page for making text stand out or for making it match editorial standards (such as setting book titles in italics). They're easy to use, but use them sparingly; too much of this stuff makes text busy and hard to read.

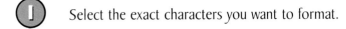

Select the exact characters you want to format.

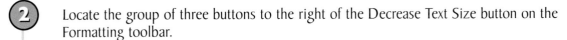

Locate the group of three buttons to the right of the Decrease Text Size button on the Formatting toolbar.

Click a button to format the selected characters: the **Bold** button, **Italic** button, or **Underline** button.

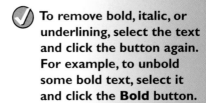
To remove bold, italic, or underlining, select the text and click the button again. For example, to unbold some bold text, select it and click the **Bold** button.

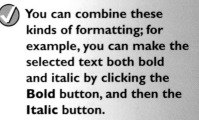
You can combine these kinds of formatting; for example, you can make the selected text both bold and italic by clicking the **Bold** button, and then the **Italic** button.

Task 17: Choosing the Color of Text

In Part 5, you learn how to choose a coordinated color scheme for your Web page—a scheme for making sure that all the colors used for text, the background, and other objects all work together. If you do that, you probably won't be choosing colors selectively for blocks of text. Still, you may find yourself wanting to give a heading or other selected text its own, unique color. Here's how.

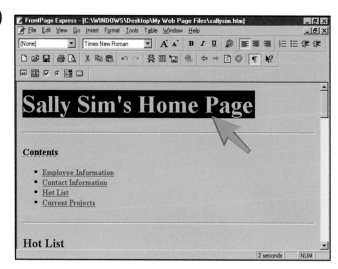

✓ If none of the colors that appear in the color dialog box appeal to you, click the dialog box's **Define Custom Colors** button, and a palette appears showing all colors possible on your PC as it is currently configured. Click the palette to create a "Custom Color," and then apply that color by clicking the square in which it appears.

 Select the exact characters for which you want to choose a color.

 Click the **Text Color** button on the formatting toolbar.

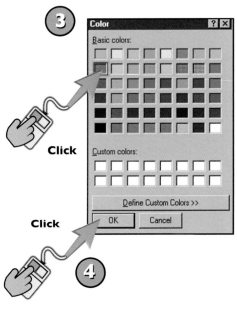

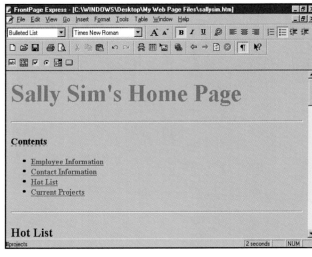

Click

Click

③ Click the colored square containing the color you want to apply. (Be careful to choose a color that will show up against the current background color.)

④ Click **OK**.

Making Links

You know links: They're the things you can click in a Web page that take your visitors somewhere else (or do other stuff, like start a file download). Although in some ways links may seem like one of the more technical aspects of a Web page, they're surprisingly easy to create. The only tricky part is deciding where you want a link to lead; the rest is a piece o' cake.

Tasks

Task 1: Exploring How Links Work

Every link has two parts: the *link source*—the object in the page that a visitor clicks to activate the link—and the *URL*—the address of the page to which that link takes the visitor. Creating links is really just a matter of creating the link source in your page, and then adding the URL behind it.

You can learn a lot more about links by studying the link sources and URLs in the pages you visit online.

When the link source is text, it usually appears underlined and in a unique color. When the link source is a picture, you can locate the link by pointing to the picture; if it's a link, the pointer becomes a pointing hand.

 Open your Web browser (Internet Explorer or Netscape Navigator) and connect to the Internet.

 Surf to a page you like that contains links.

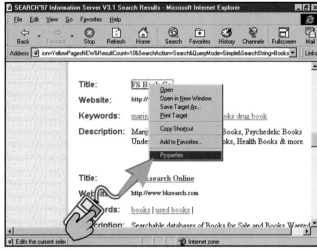

Right Click

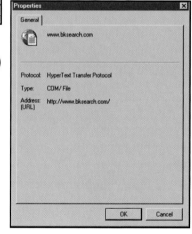

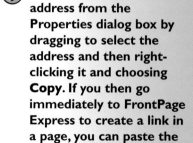

Point to a link whose link source is text, and right-click it.

Choose **Properties**. The Properties dialog box reports the address (URL) to which the link points, along with other information.

✓ You can copy a Web page address from the Properties dialog box by dragging to select the address and then right-clicking it and choosing Copy. If you then go immediately to FrontPage Express to create a link in a page, you can paste the URL into the dialog box by clicking there and pressing Shift+Insert.

Task 2: Choosing Where the Links in Your Personal Page Point

Start Here

If you used FrontPage Express's Personal Home Page Wizard to start a page (as described in Part 2), your page already contains some links: The "Hot List." But those links lead to phony addresses now. Here's how to make them point wherever you want.

1

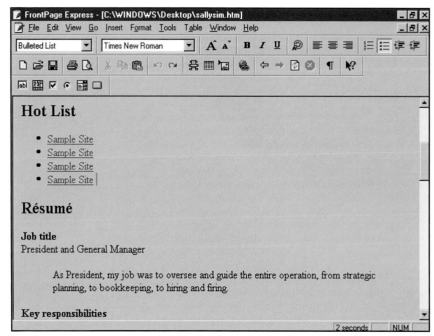

2

You can, of course, edit the link source to change it from "Sample Site" to anything you like. But sometimes when you edit link source text, you inadvertently remove the link formatting—you change it from a link source to ordinary text. If that happens to you, just make the link again as described in the first few steps of Task 3. It only takes a couple of clicks.

1   Come up with a Web site address you like. (If you need a suggestion, try `http://www.mcp.com`.)

2   Point to one of the "Sample Site" links listed in your Hot List.

Next Step

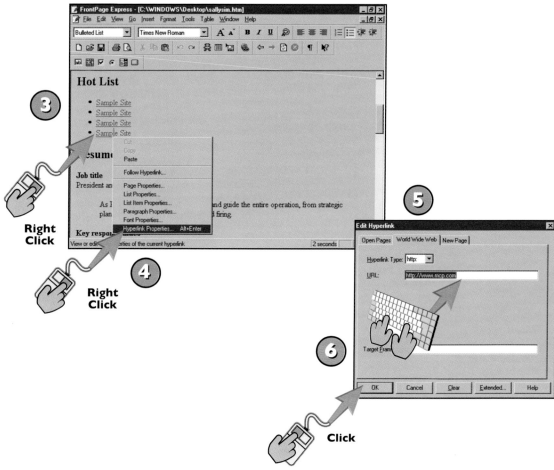

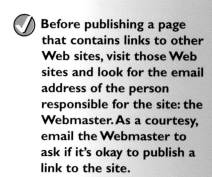

3 Right-click the **Sample Site** link.

4 Choose **Hyperlink Properties**.

5 Make sure that the **World Wide Web** tab is selected.

6 Type the complete URL in the **URL** box. Be sure to include the **http://**. Click **OK**.
The link source you pointed to in step 2 is now a link that points to an URL you chose.

✓ Before publishing a page that contains links to other Web sites, visit those Web sites and look for the email address of the person responsible for the site: the Webmaster. As a courtesy, email the Webmaster to ask if it's okay to publish a link to the site.

Task 3: Creating New Links from Scratch

In Task 2, you had a head start—the link source had already been created, so all you had to do was add the URL. Now it's time to create a link from scratch: source and URL together.

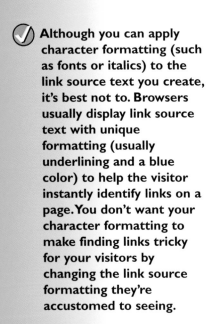

Click

Although you can apply character formatting (such as fonts or italics) to the link source text you create, it's best not to. Browsers usually display link source text with unique formatting (usually underlining and a blue color) to help the visitor instantly identify links on a page. You don't want your character formatting to make finding links tricky for your visitors by changing the link source formatting they're accustomed to seeing.

 Type and format the text that will serve as the link source.

 Select the text.

 Click the **Create or Edit Hyperlink** button on the Standard toolbar.

Next Step

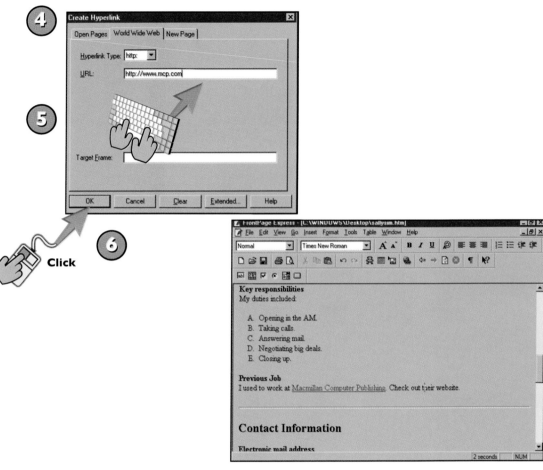

4 Make sure that the **World Wide Web** tab is selected.

5 In the box labeled **URL**, type the complete URL. Be sure to include the **http://** part at the beginning.

6 Click **OK**.

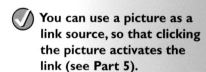

You can use a picture as a link source, so that clicking the picture activates the link (see **Part 5**).

Task 4: Linking Your Own Pages to Each Other to Make a Web Site

Ultimately, you may have more to say than can fit conveniently on a single page. Instead, you'll create a *Web site* made up of several pages linked together. Linking one of your own pages to other pages of yours is a little different—and a little easier—than linking elsewhere.

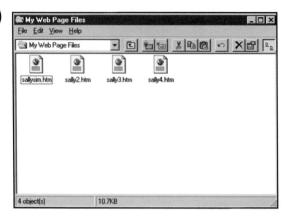

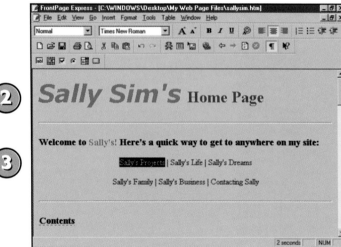

Sally Sim's Home Page

Welcome to Sally's! Here's a quick way to get to anywhere on my site:

Sally's Projects | Sally's Life | Sally's Dreams

Sally's Family | Sally's Business | Contacting Sally

Contents

✔ One good way to link pages together is to create a block of links—containing a separate link for each page—and put it at the bottom of every page. That way, your visitors can jump from any page in your Web site to any other with just one click.

① Create the Web pages that will make up your Web site, and save them all in the same folder.

② Type and format the text that will serve as the link sources.

③ Select the text of one link source.

Next Step

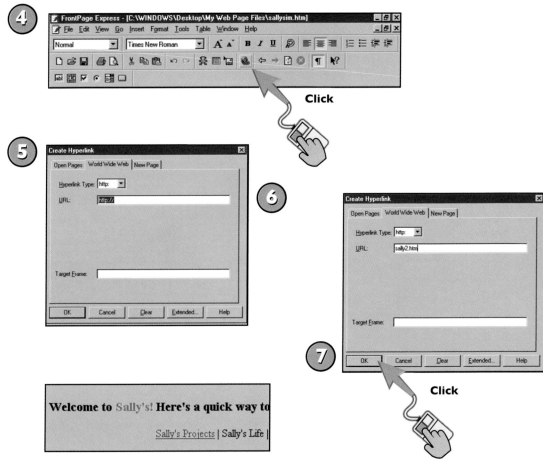

Click

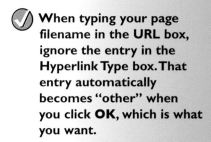

Click

Welcome to Sally's! Here's a quick way to

Sally's Projects | Sally's Life |

④ Click the **Create or Edit Hyperlink** button on the Standard toolbar.

⑤ Make sure that the **World Wide Web** tab is selected.

⑥ In the box labeled **URL**, type the complete filename of the page file to which this link points (including the **.htm** part). Do not put "http://" at the beginning.

⑦ Click **OK**.

✓ When typing your page filename in the URL box, ignore the entry in the Hyperlink Type box. That entry automatically becomes "other" when you click **OK**, which is what you want.

✓ When you publish this Web site, it will be important that you store all of your Web page files in the same directory on the Web server.

End Task

Task 5: Linking to a Particular Spot in a Page

Links don't always lead to other pages or files. In a long or complex page, a link may lead to another part of the same page where the link is. If you created the **Personal Home Page in Part 2,** you may have noticed that the top of the page contains a "Contents" list of links, each of which jumps to a particular section of the page. That Contents list works because of *bookmarks* like those you're about to create.

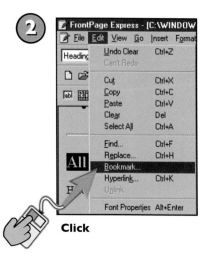

Click

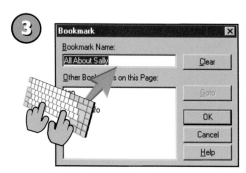

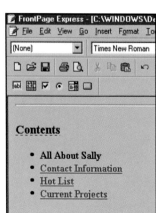

(✓) In step 3, the text you selected in step 1 appears automatically as the bookmark name. You can leave that text alone and let it serve as the name, or change it to another name. Changing the bookmark name has no effect on the text in the page.

① Select text at the spot where you want a bookmark.

② Click **Edit**, and then choose **Bookmark**.

③ Type a name for this bookmark and click **OK**.

④ Create the link source for a link to that bookmark.

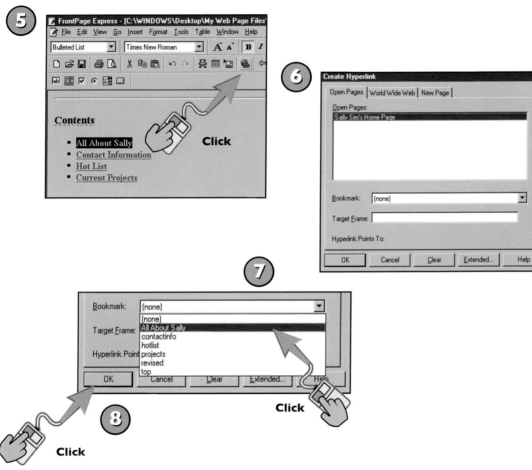

In FrontPage Express, a dashed line appears underneath text to which a bookmark is attached, so you can tell at a glance where your bookmarks are located. The underlining does not show up when the page is viewed through a browser.

FrontPage Express calls the spots you can link to within a page "bookmarks." But different terms for the same thing are used outside of FrontPage. In some other Web authoring programs, bookmarks are called "targets," and in HTML authoring (see Part 9) they're called "anchors."

5 Select the link source, and then click the **Create or Edit Hyperlink** button on the Standard toolbar.

6 Click the **Open Pages** tab.

7 Open the **Bookmark** list, and choose the bookmark's name.

8 Click **OK**.

Task 6: Linking to Files So Your Visitors Can Download Them

You may have content that you want to offer your visitors, but don't want to turn into a Web page. For example, if you have a long story, report or other document in a word processing file, it may be better to offer that file for downloading instead of turning it into a Web page (or series of Web pages). You can offer any kind of computer file for downloading—documents, sound clips, pictures, and so on.

✓ In order to use a file you provide, the visitor must have the right program. For example, if you publish a Word file, the visitor must have a program that can display (or convert) Word files in order to view it. There's not much you can do about this except to try to offer only popular, widely used file types, such as Word for documents, .avi for video clips (see Part 5), or .wav for sound clips.

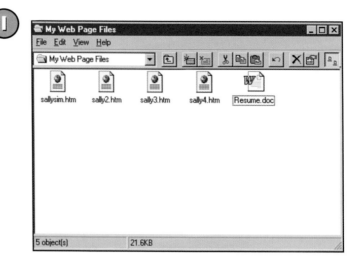

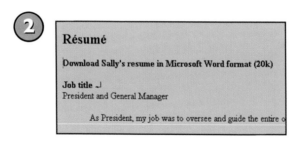

① Get the file you want to link to, and move or copy it to the folder where your Web page files are stored.

② In the Web page, type and format the text that will serve as the link source.

③ Select the text of the link source.

Click

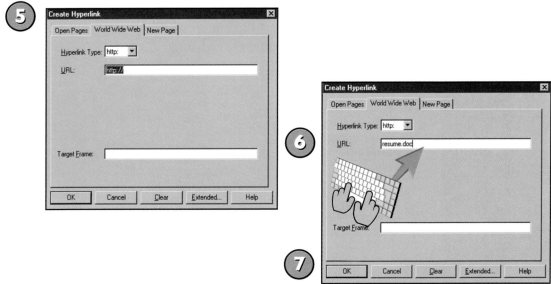

In the link source text (or right next to it), it's courteous to tell your visitors the file type (so they can tell whether it's a file they're equipped to view) and size (so they can guesstimate how long it will take to download at the speed of their Internet connection).

✓ When you publish this Web site, it will be important that you store all of your Web page files in the same directory on the Web server.

④ Click the **Create or Edit Hyperlink** button on the Standard toolbar.

⑤ Make sure that the **World Wide Web** tab is selected.

⑥ In the box labeled **URL**, type the complete filename of the file. Do not put "http://" at the beginning.

⑦ Click **OK**.

End
Task

Task 7: Linking to Your Email So Visitors Can Contact You

Near the bottom of the **Personal Home Page** example, and in many pages you'll see online, a signature appears. A *signature* is just text telling visitors who created (or manages) the page. Usually, a signature includes a *mailto link*, a link that points to the email address of the Web page author. If you add a signature and mailto link to your page, when a visitor clicks that link, his email program opens a new message, automatically pre-addressed to you.

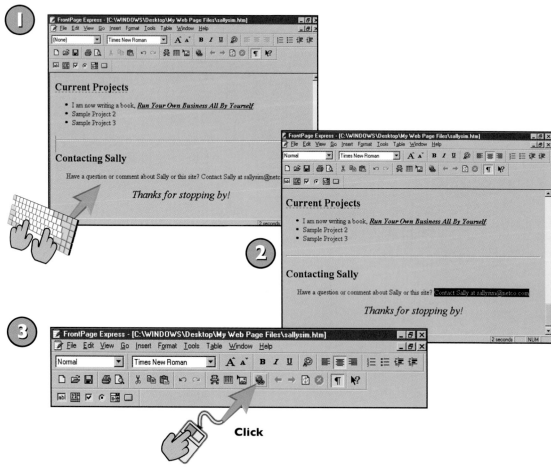

Click

1. Near the bottom of your page (or in another easy-to-find spot), type a signature message like the one shown.

2. Select some text in the message—your name or email address—to serve as a link source for the mailto link.

3. Click the **Create or Edit Hyperlink** button on the Standard toolbar.

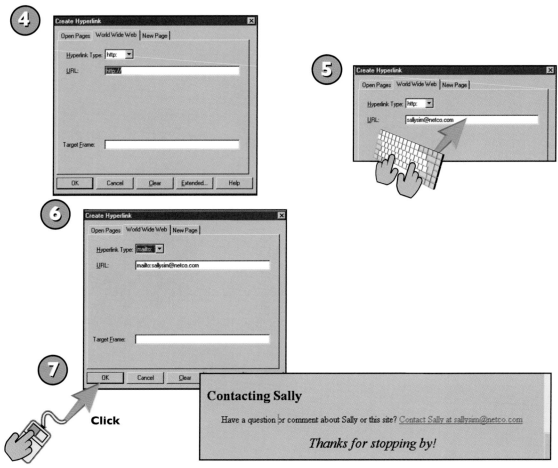

Contacting Sally

Have a question or comment about Sally or this site? Contact Sally at sallysim@netco.com

Thanks for stopping by!

(4) Make sure that the **World Wide Web** tab is selected.

(5) In the box labeled URL, type your complete email address. Do not put "http://" or anything else at the beginning.

(6) In the Hyperlink Type box, choose **mailto:**. The word "mailto" appears right before your email address.

(7) Click **OK**.

(✓) The link source of a mailto link need not show your exact email address, because most visitors' email programs will use the right address automatically when they click the link. However, some visitors use Internet software that doesn't support mailto links; they see the link source, but nothing happens when they click it. So always include your exact email address somewhere in the signature (if you really want to be contacted).

End Task

Task 8: Checking that Links Go Where They're Supposed To

When you've created links that lead from your page to other pages online, the only way to make absolutely sure that links lead where they're supposed to is to test the links online, *after* you've published your page. Still, you can do a pretty reliable pre-publishing link check at any time right from within FrontPage Express.

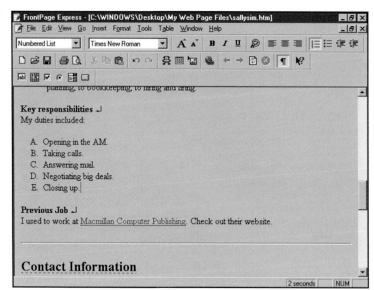

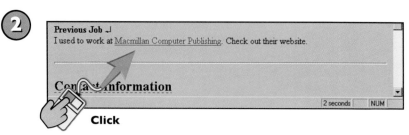

Click

Connect to the Internet, open FrontPage Express, and open the page file whose links you want to test.

Point to a link you want to test, and click so that the edit cursor appears there.

Next Step

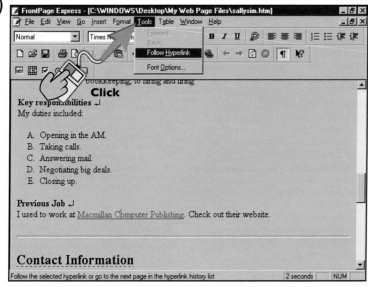

Click

Key responsibilities ↵
My duties included:

A. Opening in the AM.
B. Taking calls.
C. Answering mail.
D. Negotiating big deals.
E. Closing up.

Previous Job ↵
I used to work at <u>Macmillan Computer Publishing</u>. Check out their website.

Contact Information

Click

3️⃣ Click **Tools**.

4️⃣ Choose **Follow Hyperlink**.

✅ You don't need to connect to the Internet to test links to bookmarks or to files on your **PC** (such as other pages within a Web site you're creating but have not yet published). You can test those just by opening the page file in your browser and trying the links offline.

✅ Even if your links work, be careful to test them again online after you have published your page.

End Task

PART 5

Adding *Style* to Your Pages

You put the meat of your message in a Web page's text. Once that goal is met, you can consider what will make your page more exciting to look at, more attractive, or more fun. In this part, you'll explore the ways you can give your page some serious style, including choosing colors, adding pictures, and even adding animation and sound.

A word of caution first: A busy, over-styled Web page is an eyesore, a document that may actually be inferior to a less jazzy—but clearer—page. Although the number of jazzed up Web pages grows, most visitors hit a page for its text content, not its style. The style is a nice addition, but if it overwhelms the substance, you may lose more visitors than you gain.

And although colors, backgrounds, and horizontal lines have no real impact on page's performance, every picture, sound, or animation you add to a page lengthens the time it takes the page to fully materialize on a visitor's screen. You know from your own surfing trips how frustrating a slow Web page is, especially when it's slow just because it has too many pictures.

Dress up your page, by all means. Just don't overdo it.

Tasks

Task 1: Choosing Text Colors & Background Colors

Picking colors for various objects is not a series of separate tasks, but one job. You're creating a *color scheme*, a group of colors that both contrast and complement one another. In creating your scheme, you pick the color for the background, text, links, *visited links* (links the visitor has used already), and *active links* (links the visitor has just clicked, but which still appear onscreen briefly while the link is being activated).

✓ Instead of a solid color background, you can use an image as a background (see Task 16).

✓ Be careful that all of your selected text and link colors stand out against the background. For example, if you select a dark background color, all of the text colors must be light so the text will be legible.

Start Here

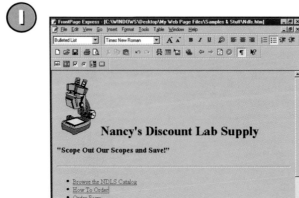

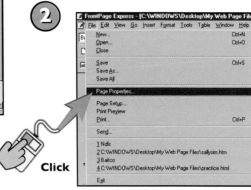

Click

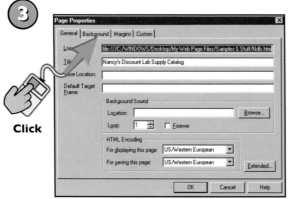

Click

Open the page whose colors you want to choose.

Click **File**, and then choose **Page Properties**.

Click the **Background** tab.

Next Step

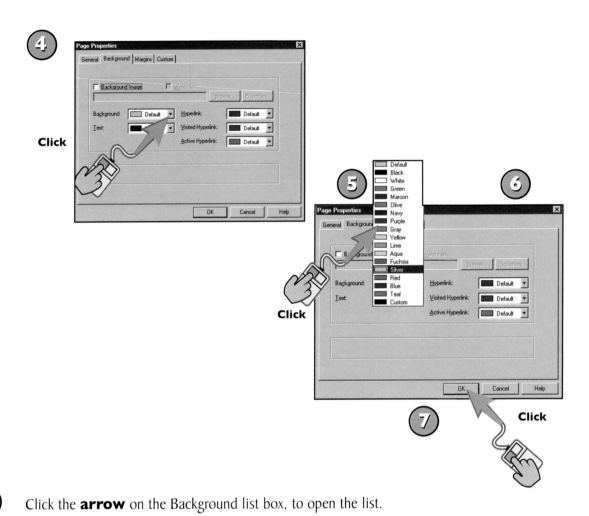

Click the **arrow** on the Background list box, to open the list.

Click the color you want to use for the background.

Repeat steps 4 and 5 for the other color lists.

Click **OK**.

Choosing Default from a color list assigns no color. It allows the color for that object to be determined by the color settings in the visitor's browser. Because the color the browser chooses might not show up properly with other colors you've selected, never pick Default unless you pick Default for *all* colors in the page.

In the color lists, the Custom choice opens a dialog box in which you can create and select a different color from those already shown in the list.

Task 2: Adding Lines to Divide Up a Page

Horizontal lines help divide up a page visually. Used between a heading and the paragraph that follows it, a line can add a little extra style to a page. Lines also help divide sections of a longer page. Best of all, they're incredibly easy to add.

Start Here

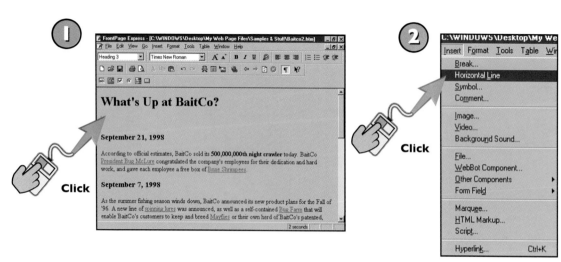

Click

Click

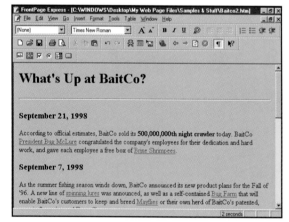

✓ You may see fancy, multicolor lines dividing some pages. These aren't real lines; they're pictures, used like lines. You can find these pictures in clip art libraries (see Task 4) in categories with names like "Bars" or "Rules," and you insert them like any other picture (see Task 8).

 Click in your page at the spot where you want to insert the line.

 Click **Insert**, and then choose **Horizontal Line**.

Task 3: Changing the Look of a Line

Start Here

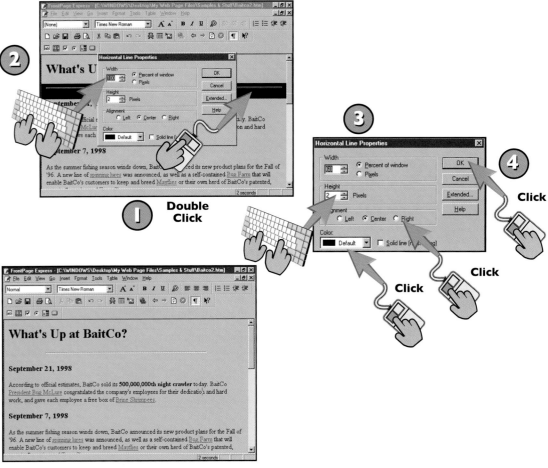

Double Click

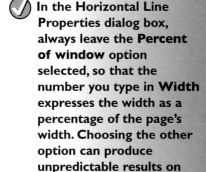

Click

Click

Click

Adding a basic horizontal line is a snap. But with just a little extra effort, you can change that line's appearance, making it thicker or thinner, making it shorter, and choosing its alignment on the page.

---

1   Double-click a line you've inserted.

2   To make the line shorter than the full width of the page, type a **Width** less than 100.

3   Type a number in **Height** to change the thickness of the line; a higher number makes a thicker line.

4   Choose an **Alignment** (**Left**, **Right**, or **Center**) and **Color** for the line, and then click **OK**.

✓ In the Horizontal Line Properties dialog box, always leave the **Percent of window** option selected, so that the number you type in **Width** expresses the width as a percentage of the page's width. Choosing the other option can produce unpredictable results on visitors' screens.

End Task

Task 4: Finding Pictures

Nearly all of the images you see in Web pages are in **GIF** file type, using the filename extension **.gif**. Some are in **JPEG (.jpg)** format, especially photographs. Any pictures used in your **Web** pages—created or borrowed—must be in one of these formats. You can create your own pictures (see Task 6), but you can also pick up great pictures from clip art libraries on **CD-ROM** or online.

✓ Some clip art you must pay for, some is free, and some is free with strings attached—for example, some sites let you use their clip art free as long as you include text next to it crediting the artist. Always read and follow all copyright notices and other usage instructions.

✓ A good way to find tons of clip art sites is to do a search with **Yahoo!** (www.yahoo.com), or **Excite** (www.excite.com), using web clip art as a search term.

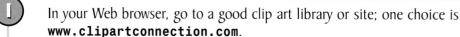

In your Web browser, go to a good clip art library or site; one choice is **www.clipartconnection.com**.

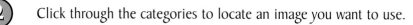

Click through the categories to locate an image you want to use.

Task 5: Copying a Picture from the Web

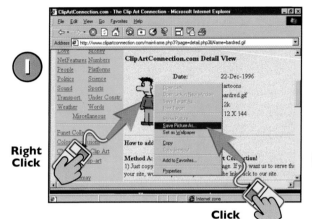

Right Click

Click

When you locate a clip art picture online you want to use, you first copy it to a folder on your PC (shown in the following steps), and then insert it on your document (as shown in Task 8).

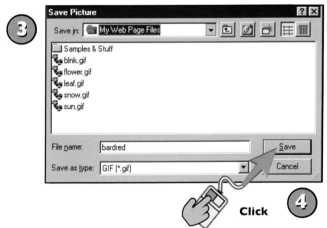

Click

1. While viewing the clip art in your browser, right-click the picture.

2. Choose **Save Picture As** (if you browse in Internet Explorer) or **Save Image As** (if your browse in Netscape Navigator).

3. Open the **Save in** list, and choose the folder that holds the Web page in which you intend to insert this picture.

4. Click **Save**.

If the picture you want to use is in a clip art library you obtained on diskette or **CD-ROM**, always copy the picture file from there to the folder where your Web page files are stored, and then insert the picture as shown in Task 8.

You can create your own
Web page pictures with
almost any draw or paint
program you may have. In
fact, Paint—the program
built in to Windows—works
just great.

Task 6: Creating Pictures

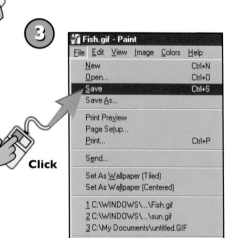

Click

Click

✓ To learn how to paint a
picture in Windows Paint,
open Paint, click **Help**, and
click **Help Topics**.

✓ To get your own
photographs into your Web
pages, scan them with a
scanner, take them to a
computer graphics shop to
be scanned, or take them
with a digital camera. Use
the scanner's or camera's
software to save the image
as a **GIF** or **JPEG** file and
store it in the same folder
as the Web page file.

1 Click Start, and then choose **Programs**, **Accessories**, and **Paint**.

2 Use Paint's tools to create your masterpiece.

3 When it's time to save your creation, click **File**, and then choose **Save**.

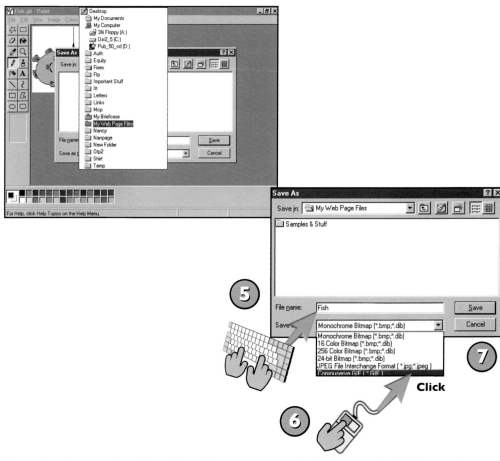

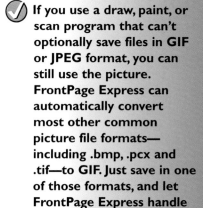

Click

If you use a draw, paint, or scan program that can't optionally save files in GIF or JPEG format, you can still use the picture. FrontPage Express can automatically convert most other common picture file formats— including .bmp, .pcx and .tif—to GIF. Just save in one of those formats, and let FrontPage Express handle the conversion.

(4) Use the **Save in** list to select the folder where you store the Web page in which you will use this picture.

(5) Type a short **File name** for your creation. (Don't type any filename extension—a period and three letters at the end.)

(6) Drop down the **Files of Type** list, and choose **CompuServe GIF (*.GIF)**.

(7) Click **Save**.

Task 7: Giving a Picture a Transparent Background

Using your draw, paint, or image-editing software, you can give your GIF pictures a "transparent" background; without a transparent background, the picture appears in the page to have a rectangular, colored background. Here's how to choose transparency in Paint:

✓ If parts of the picture you want to be visible are the same as the background color, they too become transparent when you perform step 3. To prevent this, between steps 2 and 3 click the **Select Color** button, and choose a color not used elsewhere in your picture.

✓ After you insert the picture (see Task 8), the background will not look transparent in FrontPage Express. To see your GIF as visitors will see it (with its transparent background), view the page through your browser.

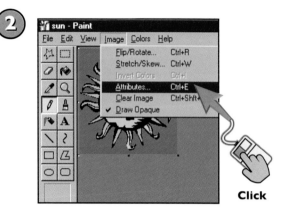

Click

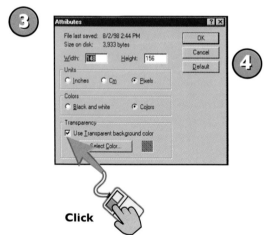

Click

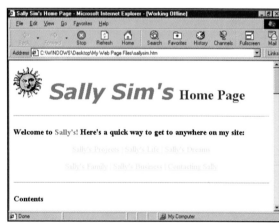

1 In Paint, open a picture you've saved in GIF format.

2 Click **Image**, and then choose **Attributes**.

3 In the Transparency section, check the check box next to **Use Transparent background color**.

4 Click **OK**.

Task 8: Putting a Picture in a Page

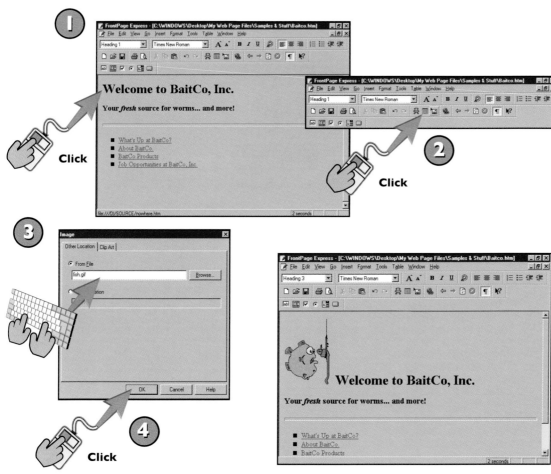

Click

Click

Click

After you have your **GIF** or **JPEG** image ready to go, just drop it in your page right where you want it. It's important to start with the picture file stored in the same folder as your Web page file. This not only makes inserting the picture easier, but also makes publishing easier, as you learn in **Part 7**.

✓ To move a picture after inserting it, just point to it, click and hold, drag to the new spot, and release. Alternatively, you can move a picture with cut and paste, just like text. Select the picture, click the **Cut** button, click in the new spot, and click the **Paste** button.

✓ If the picture you want to insert is not in **GIF** or **JPEG** format, you can still insert it by typing its filename in step 3. When you save this Web page, FrontPage Express automatically converts the file to **GIF** format.

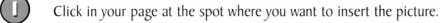

① Click in your page at the spot where you want to insert the picture.

② Click the **Insert Image** button on the Standard toolbar.

③ Type the filename of the picture, or click **Browse** to choose it from a dialog box.

④ Click **OK**.

Task 9: Changing the Size of a Picture

Suppose that after you insert a picture, you feel it's too large or too small? No problem—you can change its size right from within FrontPage Express.

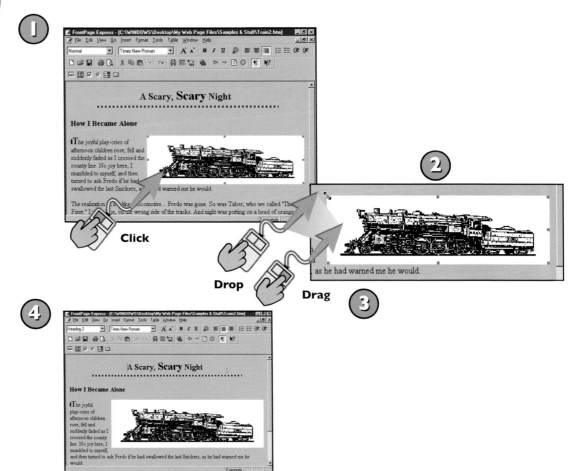

Click

Drop

Drag

When you drag a corner handle, dragging toward the center of the image makes it smaller and dragging away from the center makes it larger.

(1) Click the picture to select it. *Handles*—little squares—appear around the picture to show it's selected.

(2) Point to a handle on a corner—not a side or the top or bottom—of the picture.

(3) Click and hold on the corner handle, and drag to resize the image.

(4) Click anywhere else in the page to deselect the picture.

Task 10: Changing the Shape of a Picture

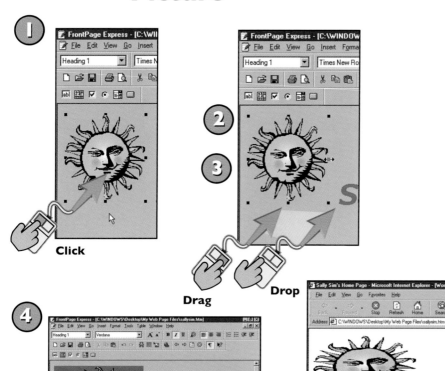

Click

Drag

Drop

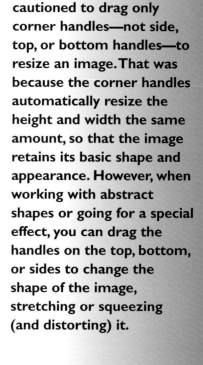

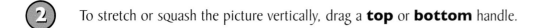

Click the picture to select it.

To stretch or squash the picture vertically, drag a **top** or **bottom** handle.

To widen or narrow the picture horizontally, drag a **side** handle.

Click anywhere else in the page to deselect the picture.

In Task 9, you were cautioned to drag only corner handles—not side, top, or bottom handles—to resize an image. That was because the corner handles automatically resize the height and width the same amount, so that the image retains its basic shape and appearance. However, when working with abstract shapes or going for a special effect, you can drag the handles on the top, bottom, or sides to change the shape of the image, stretching or squeezing (and distorting) it.

If you decide you don't like the way you changed the shape after it's too late to click the **Undo** button, you can easily restore the image to its original size and shape. Open the Appearance tab of the Image Properties dialog box (as shown in steps 1–3 of Task 11), and then remove the check mark from **Specify Size**.

Task 11: Putting a Border Around a Picture

Sometimes, you can make certain pictures look a little classier by putting a nice box border around them.

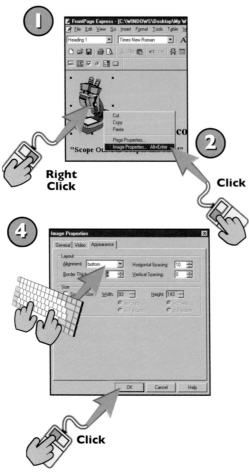

Start Here

Right Click

Click

Click

Click

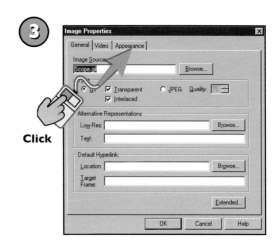

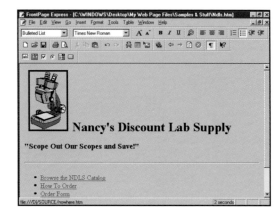

✓ Typing 4 in Border Thickness makes a nice, bold border like the one shown. A lower number makes a finer border; a higher number, a thicker one. A border thicker than 10 is probably overkill.

✓ On the Appearance tab, you have boxes for choosing Horizontal Spacing and Vertical Spacing. Raising the numbers in these boxes adds extra space between the image (or the image border, if you've added one) and whatever is next to it. Increasing vertical spacing adds space above and below the image; increasing horizontal spacing adds space to the left and right of the image.

① Right-click the picture.

② Choose **Image Properties**.

③ Click the **Appearance** tab.

④ Type a number in **Border Thickness** to add the border, and then click **OK**.

End Task

Task 12: Choosing a Picture's Alignment

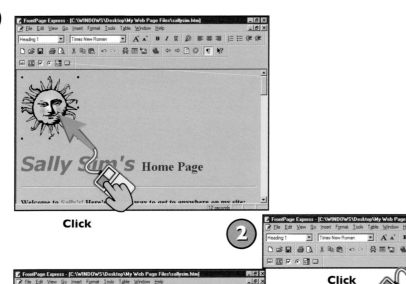

Click

By default, a picture you insert goes on the left side of the page. But you can center it or align it to the right side of the page, exactly as you do text.

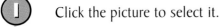

Click

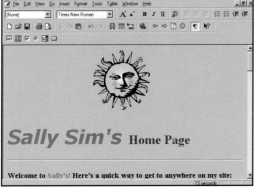

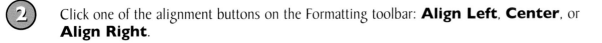

1 Click the picture to select it.

2 Click one of the alignment buttons on the Formatting toolbar: **Align Left**, **Center**, or **Align Right**.

Task 13: Controlling How Text Aligns to a Picture

When text comes right after a picture, you can choose the relationship between the text and picture. Should the text start below the image, to the right of it, or to the left of it?

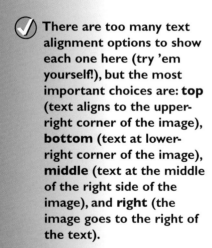

✓ There are too many text alignment options to show each one here (try 'em yourself!), but the most important choices are: **top** (text aligns to the upper-right corner of the image), **bottom** (text at lower-right corner of the image), **middle** (text at the middle of the right side of the image), and **right** (the image goes to the right of the text).

Start Here

Click

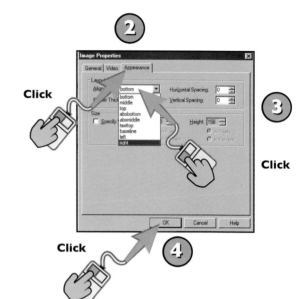

Click

Click

Click

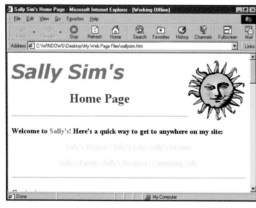

① Right-click the picture, and choose **Image Properties**.

② Click the **Appearance** tab.

③ Open the **Alignment** list, and choose the alignment you want to apply.

④ Click **OK**.

End Task

Task 14: Using a Picture as a Link

Start Here

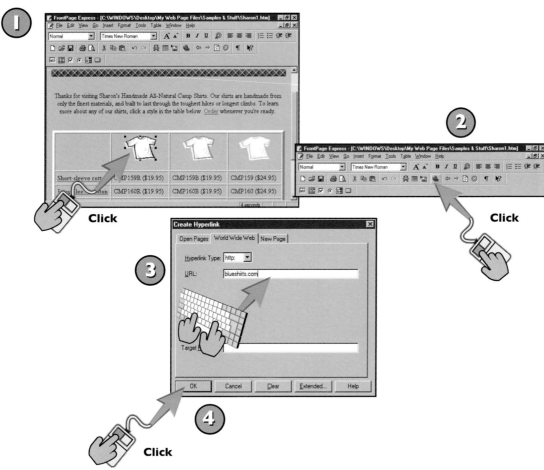

Click

Click

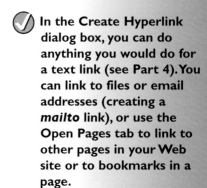

Using a picture as a *link source*—the thing a visitor clicks to activate a link (see Part 4)—is just like using text as a link source. The only difference is that you start out by selecting a picture, not text.

In the **Create Hyperlink** dialog box, you can do anything you would do for a text link (see Part 4). You can link to files or email addresses (creating a *mailto* link), or use the **Open Pages** tab to link to other pages in your Web site or to bookmarks in a page.

① Click the picture you want to make into a link.

② Click the **Create Hyperlink** button on the Standard toolbar.

③ Fill in the **URL** of the page or file to which this link leads.

④ Click **OK**.

End Task

Task 15: Creating a Times Square–Style Animated Marquee

A *marquee* is a short slice of animated text that scrolls through a Web page. The effect is like the scrolling marquee on the New York Times building in Manhattan, the one people in movies are always watching for bulletins during a crisis. Marquees are a fast way to add a little action to a page and are usually used for text you really want the visitor to notice.

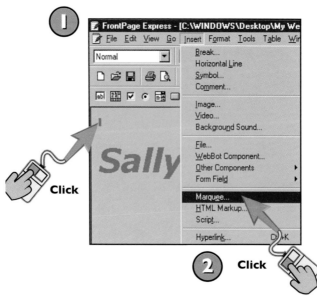

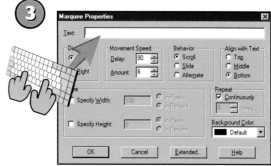

✓ At this writing, scrolling marquees are supported in Internet Explorer but not in Netscape Navigator. Navigator users will see your marquee text as regular, static text on the page.

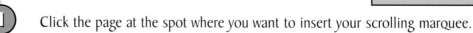

① Click the page at the spot where you want to insert your scrolling marquee.

② Click **Insert**, and then choose **Marquee**.

③ Type the text you want to see scrolling along.

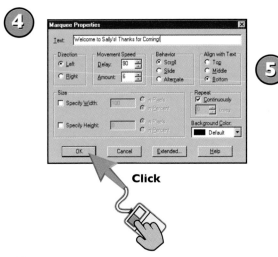

Click

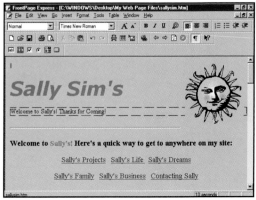

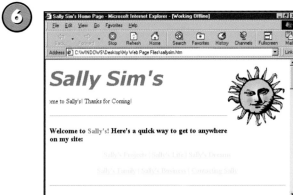

④ You may skip ahead to step 5 to use the default options for Direction, Speed, and so on, or make any changes to these settings you desire.

⑤ Click **OK**. The marquee text appears in FrontPage Express as a fixed, ordinary heading.

⑥ View the page in Internet Explorer to see the marquee scroll as it will to visitors who use Internet Explorer.

✓ To change the options or text for a scrolling marquee, just double-click the marquee to open the **Marquee Properties** box, change whatever you like, and then click **OK**.

Task 16: Adding a Picture Background

Instead of using a solid color background, as you learned to do in Task 1, you can use a picture as a background. If the picture is too small to fill the whole window in which the page appears, it is automatically tiled—repeated over and over—to fill the window.

Click

Click

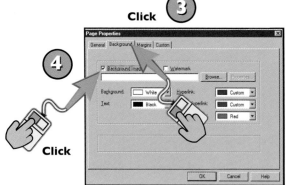

Click

Click

✓ You can get background image files that are specially designed so that, when tiled, they form a seamless texture, such as marble or wood. In clip art libraries, look for such images under categories labeled Backgrounds or Textures.

1. Store the GIF image you want for a background in the same folder as the page in which you want to use it.

2. In FrontPage Express, open the page to which you want to add a background, click **File**, and choose **Page Properties**.

3. Click the **Background** tab.

4. Click the check box next to **Background Image** to place a check mark there.

Next Step

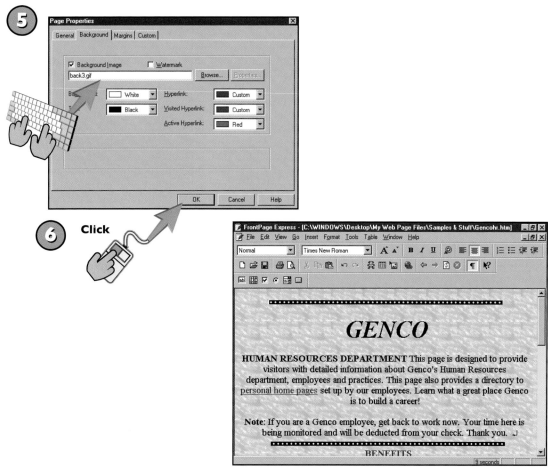

Click

5 Click in the box beneath Background Image, and type the filename of the GIF image you want to use.

6 Click **OK**.

✓ An image background automatically supercedes a background color. If you create an image background, any selection you may have made for background color is irrelevant.

✓ An image background, like any picture file, slows down the download of your page to the visitor, so avoid using very large background files. Note that a large background image slows down the page much more than a small picture tiled many times.

Task 17: Finding and Adding Animations

A special kind of GIF image file, called an *animated GIF*, plays a brief, simple animation when you view it in a Web page. You can find animated GIFs in clip art libraries online and on disk. A good way to find Web sites offering animated GIFs is to do a search with Yahoo (www.yahoo.com), Excite (www.excite.com) or another search page, using animated gif as a search term. Here's a place to start.

✓ **FrontPage Express can't play animated GIFs. View the page in Internet Explorer to see the animation.**

✓ **You can create your own animated GIFs by creating a small series (6–12) of separate GIF images, each of which is a "frame" of the animation, just like frame of film. Then you use a program to combine the frames into one animated GIF. GIF Construction Set is one such utility; check out www.mindworkshop.com.**

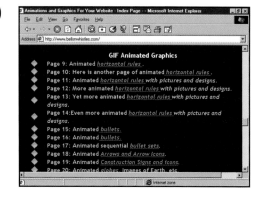

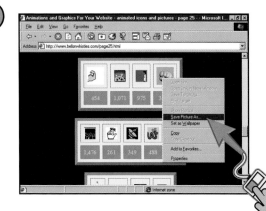

Click

1 In your Web browser, go to a clip art library containing a good selection of animated GIFs, such as **www.bellsnwhistles.com**.

2 Click through the categories to locate an animated GIF you want to use.

3 Copy the GIF to your PC and insert it in a Web page exactly as you would any GIF image (see Tasks 5 and 8).

Task 18: Finding Sound Clips

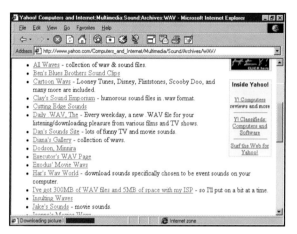

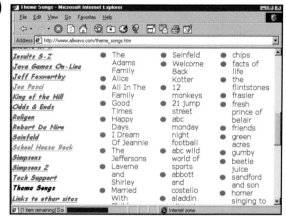

A variety of different sound file formats are used on the Web. But for Windows users, the easiest type to deal with is .wav, known as "Wave." Wave files (and other popular sound file formats, such as .au and .mid), are available in sound clip libraries online or on CD-ROM. You can download sounds to your PC, and then use them in your Web pages two ways: as background sounds (see Task 19) or as a file to which a link leads, so that a visitor can choose to play the sound by clicking the link.

1 In your Web browser, go to a sound clip archive, like those listed here in the Yahoo! directory (**www.yahoo.com**).

2 Click through the categories to locate a sound you want to use.

 You can search for archives of sound clips in much the same way you search for clip art. But sound clips are more often found on pages the sound is related to. For example, to find sound clips from your favorite TV show, you need to find a site about the TV show.

Task 19: Playing a Background Sound

A background sound is a sound clip that plays automatically when the visitor arrives at the page. You can add a background sound to a page in FrontPage Express, and choose whether that sound should play once, several times, or over and over forever.

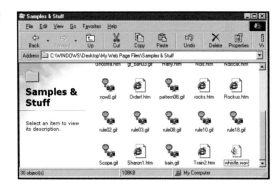

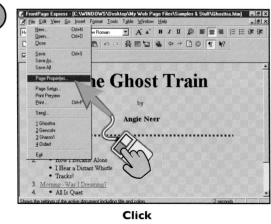

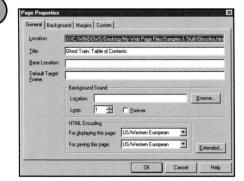

Click

At this writing, background sounds are supported in Internet Explorer, but not in Netscape Navigator. Nothing bad happens when someone uses Navigator to view a page with a background sound—they just don't hear it. So make sure your background sound doesn't contain anything essential to the page, such as a spoken welcome that's not repeated in regular text.

1 Get (or create) a short Wave file you want to use as a background sound, and store it in the same folder where the Web page is stored.

2 In FrontPage Express, open the page to which you want to add the sound, click **File**, and choose **Page Properties**.

3 Make sure the **General** tab is selected.

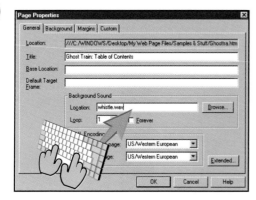

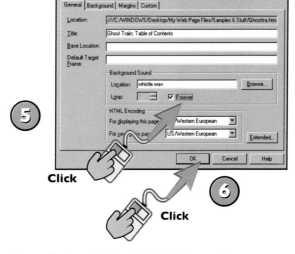

Click

Click

⑥

End
Task

④ In the Background Sound section of the dialog box, click in the box labeled **Location**, and type the filename of the Wave file.

⑤ In **Loop**, type the number of times you want the sound to repeat before stopping, or check the check box next to **Forever** to make the sound play over and over.

⑥ Click **OK**.

✓ FrontPage Express can't play background sounds. View the page in Internet Explorer to hear the sound. (Make sure your speakers are switched on.)

✓ As a rule, most sound effects or snips of speech are annoying if played more than once, so for these, type 1 in the **Loop** box. Some music clips or other sounds may be nice if kept playing; for them, you can click the **Forever** check box to play the sound continuously.

PART 6

Creating Tables and Forms

Web pages offer lots of tools for organizing content in attractive ways: headings, lists, indentation, alignment, horizontal lines, and wrapping around pictures. But when you have a lot of stuff—eight or more items—that fall logically into groups, a nice table is the way to go. In this part, you discover how easy it is to make tables, and to make them look great.

At the very end of this part, you get an introduction to a technique that doesn't simply organize information, but actually collects it from your visitors: a form.

Tasks

Task 1: Inserting a New Table

All you need to get started with tables is a page in progress, a rough idea of what you want to put in the table (sometimes it helps to scribble the table longhand first), and a rough idea of where you want to put it. Then you take off...

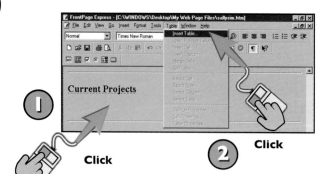

Click

Click

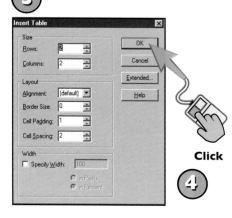

Click

Click

✓ The dashed lines that show the table borders and gridlines appear just to show you where your table is—they won't show up when the page is viewed through a browser. That's OK, a table without borders still organizes its contents into rows and columns, and can look pretty cool. But if you really want visible borders, see Task 5, "Dressing Up Tables with Borders."

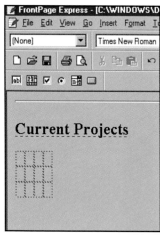

✓ Don't worry about the size of the rows and columns in the table right after you insert it. As you put text into the cells of the table, the rows and columns will expand to fit whatever you put in them.

1 Click at the spot in your page where you want to insert a table.

2 Click **Table**, and then choose **Insert Table**.

3 In **Rows** and **Columns**, choose the number of rows and columns for the table.

4 Click **OK**.

Task 2: Putting Text in Table Cells

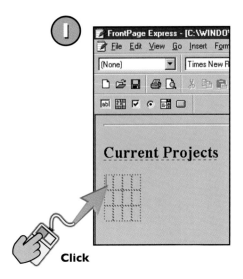

Click

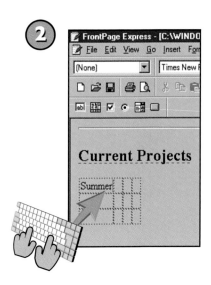

A table without content is like walls without furniture. Here's how to start filling in your new table by putting text in cells—the boxes formed by each intersection of a row and column.

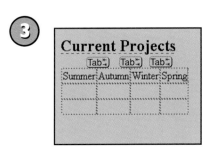

① Click in the cell in which you want to type.

② Type whatever you want.

③ Press the **Tab** key to jump to the next cell (or click in the cell you want to fill next).

✅ You can apply to text in a table any of the character formatting from Part 3, "Making Your Page Say What You Want," including fonts, sizes, bold, italic, underlining, or a special color. Making the text in all cells of the top row bold, italic, or a unique color is a nice way to create column headings that stand out.

✅ If you apply alignment (see Part 3) to text in a cell, the text is aligned relative to the cell it's in, not the page. For example, if you apply center alignment to text in a cell, the text is centered within that cell.

Task 3: Putting Pictures in a Table

Most tables are mostly text. But you can give your table panache by using a picture or two in its cells.

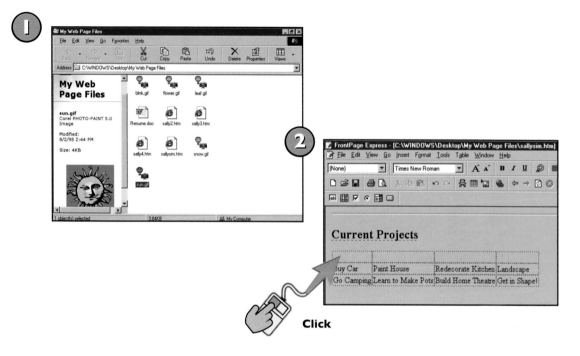

Click

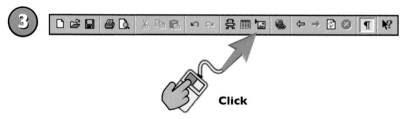

Click

✓ You can put links in a table, too. Just add to the table the text or picture you want to use as the link source, highlight that text or picture in its table cell, and create the link as usual (see Part 4, "Making Links").

1 Prepare the **GIF** or **JPEG** image you want to insert (see Part 5, "Adding *Style* to Your Pages"), and store it in the same folder as the Web page file that contains the table.

2 Click in the cell in which you want to put a picture.

3 Click the **Insert Image** button on the Standard toolbar.

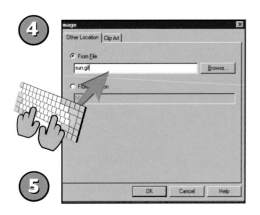

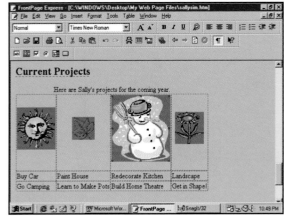

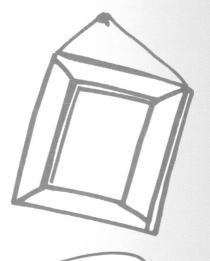

4 In **From File**, type the filename of the picture file.

5 Click **OK**.

6 Continue adding pictures to cells until you've added all the pictures for this table.

7 On each picture, drag a sizing handle to scale the picture to the size you want. The row and column sizes will have changed their size to match.

You can use any of the picture formatting techniques from **Part 5** on a picture in a table cell. To open the Image Properties dialog box to format a picture in a cell, point to the picture, right-click, and choose **Image Properties** from the pop-up menu.

End Task

Task 4: Adding a Caption to a Table

Some tables need a *caption*—a descriptive title directly above or below the cells—and some don't. For your own tables, you get to choose.

Click

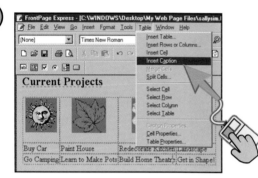

Click

✓ **FrontPage Express automatically puts captions above the table, but you can move a caption below the table. Click anywhere on the caption, click Table, and then choose Caption Properties. A dialog box appears, giving you two choices for caption placement: Top of Table and Bottom of Table.**

① Click anywhere in the table whose caption you want to add.

② Click **Table**, and then choose **Insert Caption**.

③ Type your caption. It appears above the table.

Task 5: Dressing Up Tables with Borders

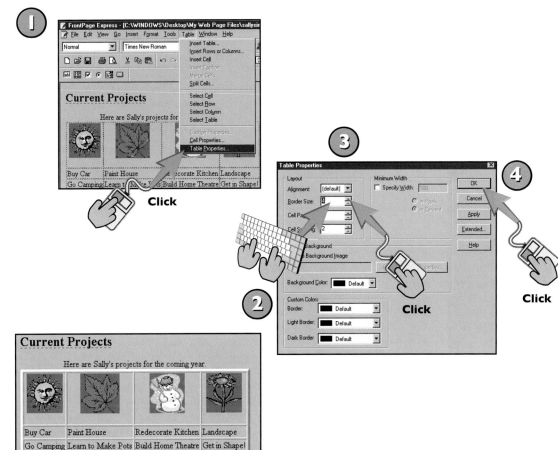

Click

Click

Click

So far, your table does a great job of lining up its content in rows and columns, but it lacks the nice grid of lines—and box all around—that delineate the content and make the table look sharp.

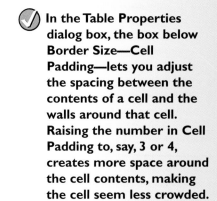

In the Table Properties dialog box, the box below Border Size—Cell Padding—lets you adjust the spacing between the contents of a cell and the walls around that cell. Raising the number in Cell Padding to, say, 3 or 4, creates more space around the cell contents, making the cell seem less crowded.

1. Click anywhere in the table, click **Table**, and then choose **Table Properties**.

2. Click the box next to **Border Size**.

3. Type a number for the width of the borders. For example, type **4** to create a border 4-pixels wide. The higher the number, the thicker the border.

4. Click **OK**.

Task 6: Choosing Custom Border Colors

A table border is not one line, but three lines used together to create a 3D effect: a basic border line, a "light border" (a highlight on the top of horizontal lines and on the left side of vertical lines) and a "dark border" (a shadow on the bottom of horizontal lines and on the right side of vertical lines). You can pick the color for each part of the border.

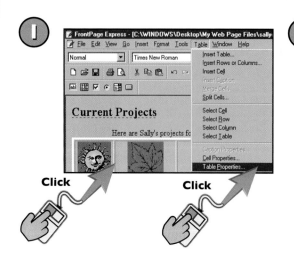

Click   **Click**

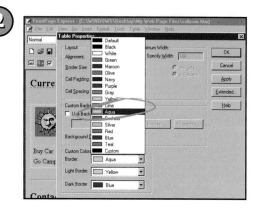

✓ To experiment with borders, border colors, and anything else in the Table Properties dialog box, make any changes in the dialog box, and then click the **Apply** button instead of OK. The changes are made in the table, but the Table Properties dialog box remains open, so you can try different settings without having to re-open it. Keep experimenting, clicking **Apply** each time, and then click **OK** when you see what you want to keep.

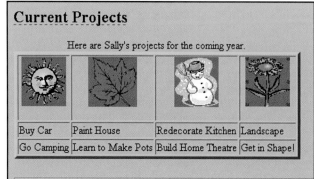

1 Click anywhere in the table, click **Table**, and then choose **Table Properties**.

2 In the **Custom Colors** section, choose a color from each of the three lists: **Border**, **Light Border**, and **Dark Border**.

Task 7: Choosing a Background for a Table

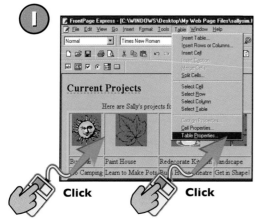

①

Click   Click

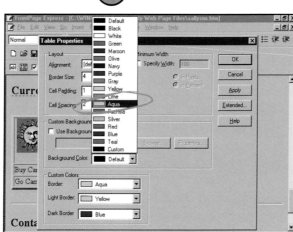

②

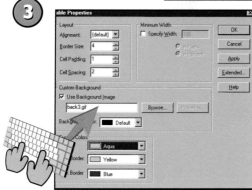

③

Unless you add a background to a table, the page's background color or image shows through the table (but does not obscure the table's content or borders). But a table can have its own background, different from that of the page, to make the table—and more important, its contents—really stand out.

✓ If you choose both a background image and a background color, the color is irrelevant—a background image overrides a background color.

✓ You can use a different background for a selected cell or cells than for the rest of the table; for example, you can give the top row its own unique background color or image to make column headings stand out. In step 1, click in a cell, click Table, and then choose **Select Cell, Select Row,** or **Select Column.** When you perform steps 2 and 3, the background you create is applied only to the selected cells.

① Click anywhere in the table, click **Table**, and then choose **Table Properties**.

② To add a solid color background, open the list next to **Background Color** and choose a color.

③ To add a picture background instead of a background color, click the check box next to **Use Background Image**. Then type the name of the GIF image file to use.

Task 8: Creating an Interactive Form

A *form* is a page (or part of a page) that collects information from your visitors by prompting them to select options from lists, check boxes, and more. You've seen and used forms on the Web.

This *Easy* book can't really show you how to do forms in a Web page—there's no such thing as an easy form. Creating the part of a form you see is pretty easy. But a form also needs a script, a behind-the-scenes program, for collecting and processing the data visitors enter in your forms—and scripts are not for beginners. This task demonstrates how to build the visible form; after building a form (or better yet, before), talk to your server administrator (see Part 7, "Publishing Your Page Online") about having a script written to make your form function.

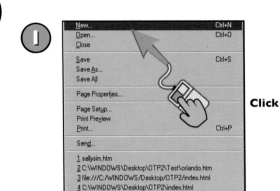

Click

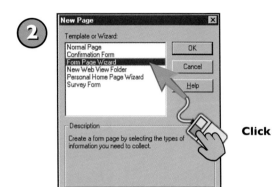

Click

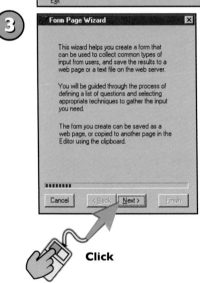

Click

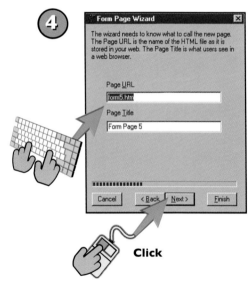

Click

1 Open FrontPage Express, click **File**, and choose **New**.

2 Click **Form Page Wizard**, and then click **OK**.

3 Click **Next**.

4 Type a filename and title, as you would for any page, and then click **Next**.

Next Step

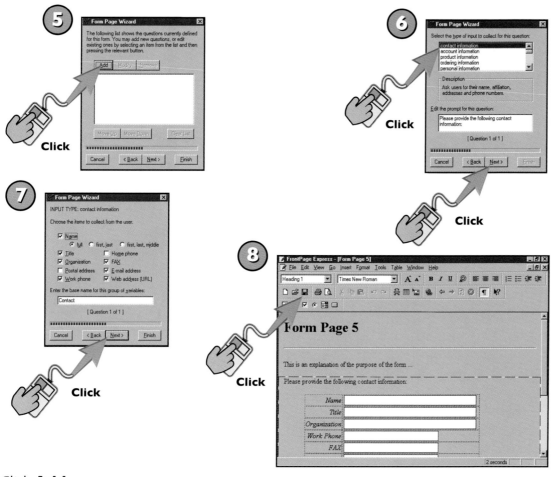

Instead of using the Form Page Wizard to create a form page, you can use the buttons on the Forms toolbar to insert *form fields*—list boxes, check boxes and so on—in any Web page. Just click in the page where you want the form field, click the button, and answer any questions FrontPage Express asks.

For a beginner, using the Form Page Wizard makes more sense than using the Forms toolbar. The Wizard helps organize and encode your form correctly, and you'll have more success with the script if you can give your server administrator a single form page requiring a script, instead of a more complex page that you may want to continue changing after the script has been completed.

You can edit the new page any way you like, formatting or adding text, adding pictures, and more. Just be careful not to delete the form fields.

(5) Click **Add**.

(6) Click **contact information**, and then click **Next**.

(7) Check or clear check boxes to select the types of contact information you want the form to collect, and then click **Finish**.

(8) Save the new page.

PART

Publishing Your Page Online

A play is not lines on a page. Even after it's all written and printed, it does not officially become a play until an audience sees it on stage.

Same deal with a Web page. It's not really a Web page until it gets on the Web. In this part, you find places on the Web you can put your pages, copy—***upload***—your pages to the Web, and more.

Tasks

Task 1: Finding Space on a Web Server

To be seen through the Web, your pages must be stored on the hard disk of a Web server. So your first step is finding some Web server space where you will be permitted to put your pages. It's likely you can get some space free from the Internet Service Provider (ISP, the company you pay for Internet access) or online server (such as America Online) you use. But if you can't get free space there, you have other options to explore—described here in decreasing order of desirability.

How much server space do you need? Well, a single Web page file with text and a few pictures is usually smaller than 100 kilobytes (about 1/10th of a megabyte). So even a Web site made up of 10 or 12 different pages may fit in less than a megabyte of server space, unless your site includes a plethora of pictures or large media files, such as video clips.

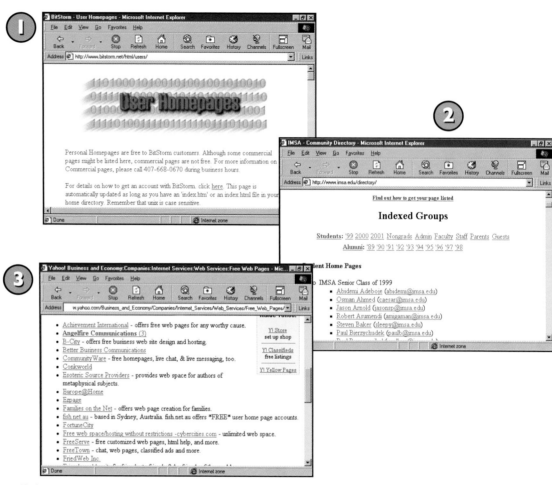

1 Call the Internet Service Provider (ISP) or the online service you use (or check out your service's Web page), and ask whether you can use some space on that company's Web server.

2 If the company you work for or school you attend has its own Web site, it may let you use some space, particularly if your page is work- or school-related.

3 Go to Yahoo! (**www.yahoo.com**) or your favorite Web search tool and enter **free web space** as a search term.

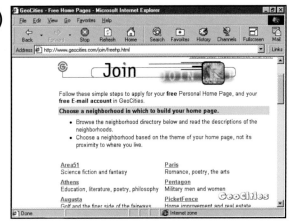

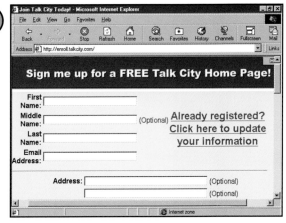

Most ISPs offer their customers a few megabytes of free server space, or will give you some for a small fee. Most charge extra if they consider your page to be a "business" or "commercial" page, because the page is expected to generate more Web traffic than a "personal" one.

GeoCities and Talk City both require special steps for putting your page online, including the requirements that you "join" the GeoCities or Talk City community first, include their ads on your pages, and follow some unusual procedures for publishing your page (different from those you learn in this book). If you want to use one of these services, explore their Web sites thoroughly to learn the rules for joining and publishing.

4 GeoCities is a company that offers free server space in exchange for the right to put advertising on your pages. Check out **www.geocities.com**.

5 Talk City is a new service offering the same basic deal as GeoCities, but a different selection of tools for doing it. Explore **www.talkcity.com**.

Task 2: Learning More About the Server You've Chosen

After you choose your server, you need to know some stuff about it before you can publish there. Your ISP may give you this info over the phone, but ISP's can be hard to talk to. Better to get this info online, if it's available there.

Start Here

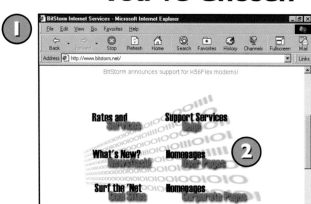

✓ The information you need for publishing includes the URL (for example, www.myserver.com), the name of the directory in which you will store your files (usually the same as your username), a password for copying your files to the server (often the same one you use to connect to the Internet), and the address of the server to which you will copy files.

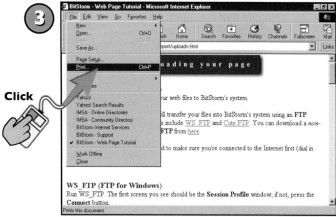

Click

✓ You need the server information, but you do not necessarily have to follow the exact publishing steps some server providers list. Except in unusual cases, you can use the steps shown in Task 4 to publish anywhere.

1 Go to the Web home page of the ISP, online service, or other organization from whom you will get server space.

2 Look for links to "User Homepages," "Uploading Files," or other links that appear to lead to information about publishing your pages.

3 Click **File** when you find it and then choose **Print** (in either Navigator or Internet Explorer) so you can refer to the printout while publishing your pages.

Task 3: Getting Ready to Publish

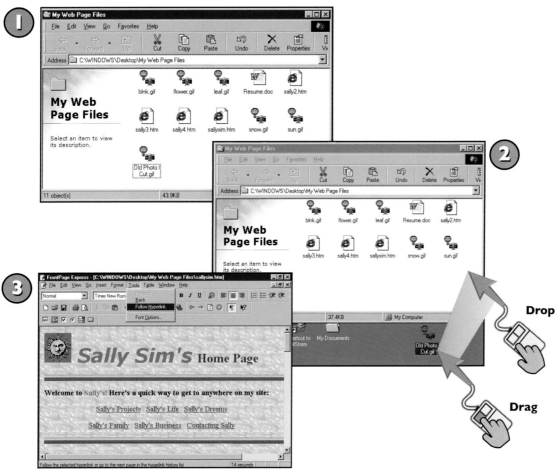

Publishing is easy. Most publishing problems happen not because publishing is hard, but because the author failed to put his or her ducks in a row before starting the publishing steps. Here's how to get those ducks lined up smartly.

Drop

Drag

① Check that all of the files making up your page or pages—HTML files, images, and any other files your page delivers through links—are all stored in the same folder.

② Delete or move from the folder anything that is NOT a part of the Web site, including any stray files or other folders.

③ Open your page and give it a final once-over, checking style, spelling, and links to bookmarks and files.

End Task

Task 4: Running the Web Publishing Wizard

Most server providers prefer that you upload—copy your Web files from your PC to the Web server—by using an Internet tool called *FTP*. If you're familiar with FTP, you can do it that way. But Microsoft's Web Publishing Wizard—which is installed automatically when FrontPage Express is installed, so you have it—can automatically publish via FTP, and in a few other ways, too. So if you don't already know FTP, there's no need to learn now—at least for publishing purposes.

✓ If your Internet setup permits you to connect to the Internet without opening your Web browser, or to close your Web browser without disconnecting from the Internet, do that when you connect for this task. You don't need your Web browser while publishing your files, just your Internet connection.

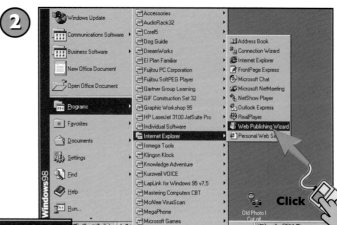

Click

Click

 Close FrontPage Express and any other programs you may have open and connect to the Internet.

 Click **Start**, click **Programs**, choose **Internet Explorer**, and choose **Web Publishing Wizard**.

 Click **Next**.

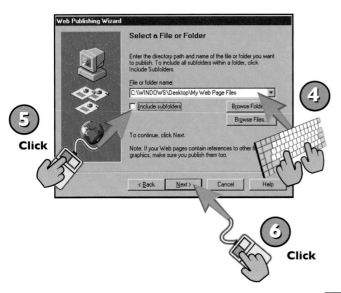

5 Click

4

6 Click

7

Click

4 Type the complete path to the folder where you store your Web page files, or click **Browse** to select it from a dialog box.

5 If a check mark appears in the **Include subfolders** box, click to remove it.

6 Click **Next**.

7 Click **New**.

If you want to publish a single file (such as an HTML File you've updated since you last published; see Task 5), add the filename to the end of the path in step 5. Only the file will be published, not all files in the folder.

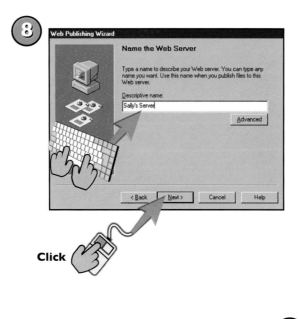

Click

Click

The URL you type in step 9 is the URL your visitors will use to visit your pages on the Web. To access your index.html file, they need only enter the URL exactly as shown in step 9. To access a page file (other than index.html), they enter the URL, a slash (/), and then the filename; for example, www.bitstorm.net/ nsnell/sally.html.

 Type a simple name to describe the Web server (this is not a technical name; type anything you want), and click **Next**.

 In the upper box, type the complete **URL** of the server and directory in which your page will be published.

 Click **Next**.

Next Step

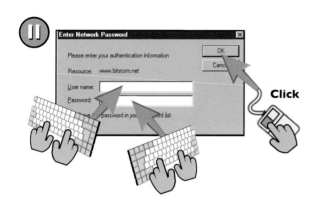

Click

Click

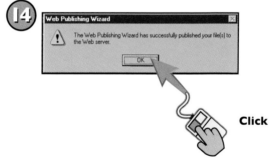

Click

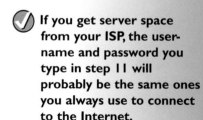

11 Type the **User name** and **Password** your server supplier gave you for uploading files, and then click **OK**.

12 Click **Finish**.

13 Wait while the Wizard uploads your pages to the server.

14 Click **OK**.

If you get server space from your ISP, the user-name and password you type in step 11 will probably be the same ones you always use to connect to the Internet.

Task 5: Updating and Editing Your Page

Fixing or updating your pages after publishing them is easier than publishing them in the first place. You must make changes to the original files on your PC and publish again. The changed files automatically replace the old ones on the server.

✓ Re-publishing is easier than publishing the first time because the Web publishing wizard remembers all the entries you made the first time for server address, the folder containing the Web page files, and so on.

✓ This procedure re-uploads your whole Web page, including pages you may not have changed. Uploading the unchanged pages adds only a few seconds, and doing so ensures that all of your changes arrive on the server. It also saves you the extra effort of moving the changed files into a separate folder for publishing.

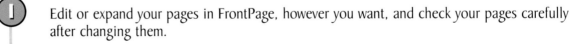

Click

1. Edit or expand your pages in FrontPage, however you want, and check your pages carefully after changing them.

2. Do steps 1, 2, and 3 of Task 4.

3. Click **Next** on the next two dialog boxes.

4. In the final dialog box, click **Finish**.

Task 6: Viewing Your Page Through the Internet

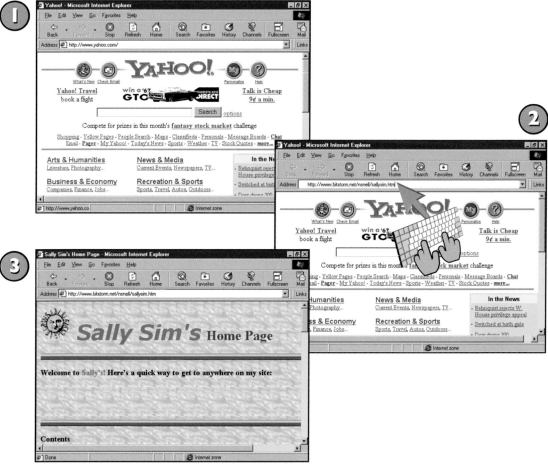

After you publish, you must test your page through the Web, viewing it exactly as your visitors will. Besides, it's fun to see it online.

1 Open your Web browser and connect to the Internet.

2 In the place in your browser where you enter a Web page address, type the Web page URL for your new page (including the filename of the HTML file you want to view), and press **Enter**.

3 Explore your page, evaluating its appearance and testing all of your links. If you find any mistakes or anything else you want to change, see Task 5.

✓ If you named your top page `index.html` (as suggested in Part 2), that page opens automatically when a visitor surfs to the server directory without specifying a filename. For example, if the user enters the URL `www.server.com/sally/` in his browser, the `index.html` file in the `sally` directory opens automatically.

Task 7: Getting Multiple Browser Programs for Testing

So your page looks great in FrontPage Express and in your own Web browser. But that does not necessarily mean it will look great to everyone. There are subtle differences among browsers, and those differences can make a page that looks great in one browser look not so great in another.

✓ If you need help with downloading programs from the Internet and installing them, see Part 10, "Discovering Other Web Authoring Tools and Techniques."

✓ If your page looks good in FrontPage Express, you can rest assured it will probably look fine in either Netscape Navigator or Internet Explorer, which means it will look fine to the majority of folks online. Still, there are small, subtle differences between even the most recent versions of these programs, so it's still smart to test in both and adjust your files as necessary.

Start Here

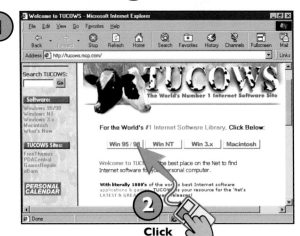

Click

Click

Click

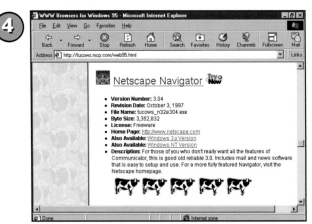

1. You can find browser programs lots of places online, but a good place to start is **tucows.mcp.com**.

2. Click the button for your system: **Win 95/98** or **Win NT**.

3. In the Browsers and accessories box, click **Browsers**.

4. Scroll through the list and use the links provided to learn about and download a variety of browsers you don't already have.

Next Step

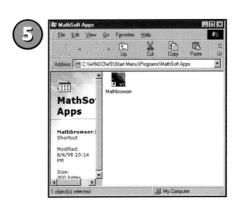

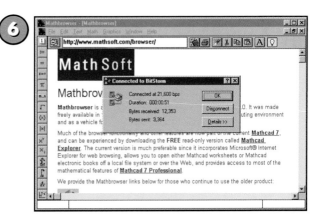

If you can figure out how to open local files (Web pages stored on your hard disk) in a particular browser—which is sometimes tricky—you can test pages offline by opening the page files in your browser.

When you install some browsers, they may try to make themselves your default browser—the one that opens automatically when you open a Web page file (see Part 2, "Building Your First Web Page"). If an unwanted browser makes itself the default, you can usually restore your original browser to its "default" status by reinstalling it.

5 Install each browser according to its instructions.

6 Connect to the Internet, and open the new browser.

7 Use the browser to surf to your page, and evaluate the page's appearance.

8 If you see major flaws that would make the page impossible to read, adjust the page in FrontPage Express, re-test in the new browser offline, and republish as described in Task 5.

End Task

Task 8: Getting Your Own *Domain*

If you simply take some space on someone else's server, your page won't have the sort of catchy address that gives you a Web identity. Instead, your page's address is expressed as a directory on the server; for example, `www.serviceco.com/sallysim/`.

☑ When typing your proposed domain in step 3, don't precede it with the "http://" or "www" part. These are part of a typical Web site address, but not really part of the domain. For example, if you want your Web site address to be `http://www.wild.com`, just type `wild.com` in step 3.

☑ The final part of the domain name can be `.com` (commercial site, the most common), `.org` (organization, like a foundation), `.edu` (educational institution), or `.net` (network). If you're not sure what to use, that makes you a `.com`.

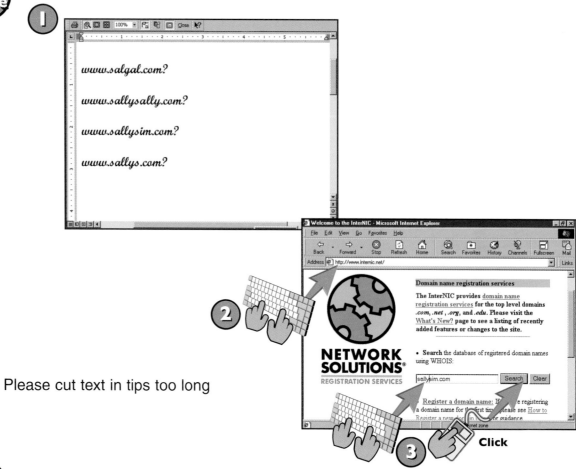

Please cut text in tips too long

1 Think about what you want your Internet domain to be; for example, www.sallysim.com.

2 Visit the Web site of InterNIC, the official organization that registers Internet domains, at `www.internic.net`.

3 In the Search box on the InterNIC top page, type the domain you chose in step 1, and click **Search**.

Most ISPs will register a domain for around $50. In addition to the setup fee, the ISP will collect an additional $70 from you to pay a required registration fee to InterNIC. That pays for your domain for two years; after that, you must pay InterNIC $35 per year to keep the domain.

You can register your domain yourself (saving the ISP's setup fee, but not the $70 due to InterNIC) by filling in the forms provided on InterNIC's Web site. However, registering a domain yourself requires technical knowledge about the Internet and the server that's probably beyond the technical ambitions of an *Easy* reader. Pay the fifty bucks and let the geeks do it for you.

4 If you get **No Match** for the domain, proceed to step 5. (If InterNIC displays a report about the domain owner, it's taken. Return to step 1, and use a different name.)

5 Contact a company that sets up domains and ask your ISP to register for you, or find another service by using a tool like Yahoo! to search for **domain registration service**.

PART 8

Announcing Your Page

Once your page or site is up on the Web, folks won't find it by osmosis. You need to get the word out so they can find you.

Of course, the scale of your Web site promotion efforts should match the ambitions of your page. If your page is just a personal home page for family, friends, and the occasional passing stranger, much of what you discover in this part would be overkill. But most people who publish Web sites do so because they want to be found by as many Web visitors as may have an interest in the site. Here's how to pull 'em in.

Tasks

Before beginning to promote your site, you should do a little surfing to locate the pages where you might want your page featured. Certainly the list includes the major search engines such as Yahoo!, Excite, and Alta Vista, but it also includes smaller directory pages that feature links to pages covering the same topic yours covers.

Most of the search engines have their own programs, called "crawlers" or "spiders," that automatically search the Web and add new sites, using each site's title and contents to automatically determine which subject categories to list it in. But a few require you to manually add your site; you learn how in Task 2.

Task 1: Finding Places to Promote Your Site

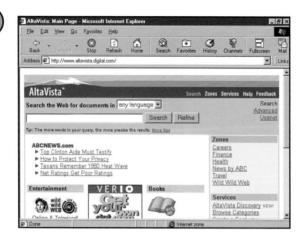

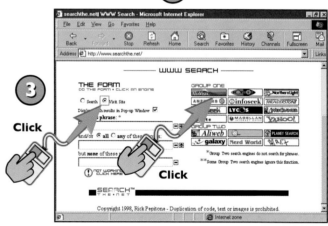

Click

Click

Visit each of the major search tools, and look for links to information about adding or "suggesting" a new site.

You can gain one-stop access to all of the major search pages by going to **www.searchthe.net**.

Click the **Visit Site** choice, and then click the button for the search page you want to visit.

Next Step

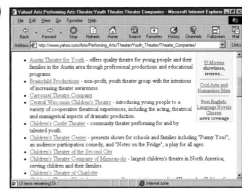

For any topic your page is related to, do a search to find pages covering that topic.

Some of those pages will include directories of links to related sites.

Send email to the Webmaster of sites containing directories asking to have your site added to the list.

The search tools with crawlers will find your page within a few weeks after you publish it. But the pages containing subject-specific directories rarely have crawlers; if you want to get listed there, you need to contact the Webmaster.

Task 2: Listing Your Page in the Yahoo! Directory

Yahoo! is the most popular directory on the Web. It's also one that does not catalog the Web automatically—you must add your site to Yahoo! to ensure that searchers find your site when doing a Yahoo! search on a term that's related to your site's contents.

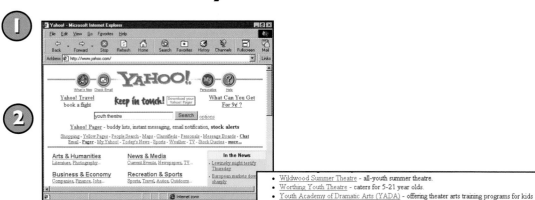

Click

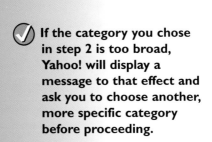 If the category you chose in step 2 is too broad, Yahoo! will display a message to that effect and ask you to choose another, more specific category before proceeding.

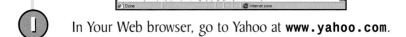

(1) In Your Web browser, go to Yahoo at **www.yahoo.com**.

(2) Use Yahoo!'s search box, or browse through its category listings, to go to a category in which your site belongs.

(3) Scroll to the bottom of the page on which your selected category list appears and click **Suggest a Site**.

(4) Read the Suggest a Site page for tips on properly listing your page with Yahoo!

Next Step

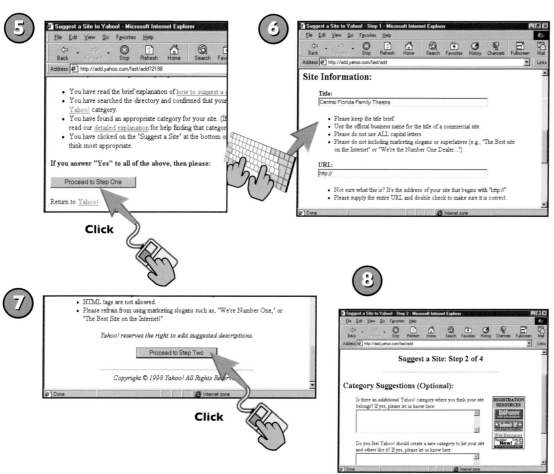

Click

Click

5 Scroll to the bottom of the Suggest a Site page and click **Proceed to Step One**.

6 Scroll down to the **Site Information** form, and type the title and URL of your page or site, plus a brief description.

7 At the bottom of the Suggest a Site page, click **Proceed to Step Two**.

8 Continue through steps 2, 3, and 4, filling in all information requested and clicking the button at the bottom of the page to proceed to each new step.

✅ The description you type in step 6 will appear in the search results whenever someone's Yahoo! search finds your page. Word it carefully to help searchers determine whether your page contains what they want. Be sure also to include in the description keywords related to the page's topic.

End Task

Task 3: Listing Your Page in the Excite Directory

Listing your page on Excite is much simpler than doing so in Yahoo!, for a simple reason. Excite uses a program to search through each site's pages, using the page's contents to determine which categories to list it in. So all you have to do is let Excite know where your site is—the program does the rest.

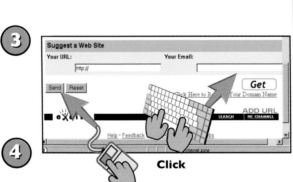

Click

Click

✓ After you manually add your site to Yahoo! or Excite, it probably won't show up right away. Typically, it takes about two weeks for your site to show up in the listings.

1 In your Web browser, go to Excite at **www.excite.com**.

2 Scroll to the bottom of the page and choose **Add URL**.

3 Fill in the **URL** of your page (or top page of your site) and your **Email** address, so Excite can contact you if necessary.

4 Click **Send**.

End Task

Task 4: Checking Out the Site Submission Services

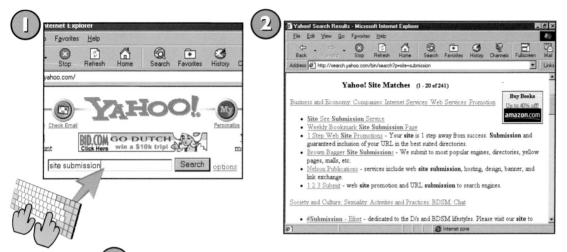

You can promote your site effectively by simply adding it to Yahoo! and the directories on a few related pages, and then waiting for the crawlers to get you listed in most other search tools. But if you really want to get the word out, there are commercial "site submission" services, sometimes also known as "web promotion" firms, that will submit your site to all the major search tools, plus hundreds of other directories. The fee for the service ranges from under $10 to over $100.

1 In the box at the top of the main Yahoo! page (**www.yahoo.com**), type **site submission** and click **Search**.

2 Read the descriptions in the search results to find sites that offer site submission.

3 Visit the sites to learn what the service offers (and what it costs).

✓ Browsing the Web sites of the site submission services, you can often pick up useful tips—for free— that can help you promote your site more effectively.

✓ There are also site-submission software packages you install on your **PC**. Check out a product called **Submissions** at www.submissions.com.

Task 5: Adding Your Web Address to Ads, Letterheads, and More

Some of the best places to publicize your page are not online, but off—there's a reason all those big companies are putting their Web site addresses in their billboards, newspaper ads, and TV commercials. Here are a few ideas...

✓ Wherever you can do so without disrupting the design of your printed publications, print the **URL** in a bright, unique color to make it stand out—just the way it does online.

✓ These days, it's not necessary to include the prefix "http://" when showing your **URL** in print. That's great, because leaving off the prefix makes the **URL** look shorter, less technical, and more friendly.

New Web Site!

SimCo Industries, Inc.

SimCo has a new Web site. Please visit us at

www.sallysim.com

For all your needs.

to learn about our latest products, services and

WEB SPECIALS!

 Add your Web site address to your stationery, business cards, business or personal newsletter, advertising, and so on.

 For a business site, put out a special flier to customers, announcing your Web site.

Task 6: Announcing Your Page by Email

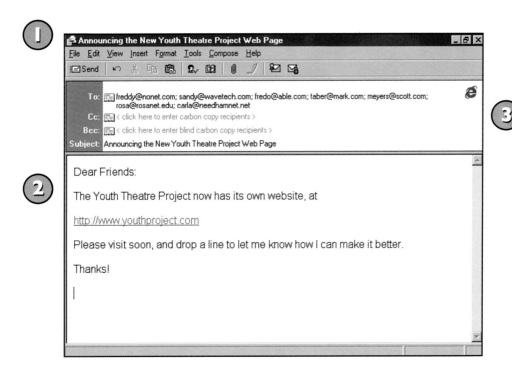

Of course, the best source of visitors for your Web page is the pool of folks already online, and you can reach them most effectively using email. An email announcement to friends, clients, or customers is a great way to inaugurate a new Web site.

✓ Be sure to type a space, or press **Enter**, right after the URL. The URL will then appear to most recipients (except those whose email programs do not support this feature) as a "live" link they can click—right in the message—to go straight to your site.

✓ Email is "letterhead" too. Folks with their own Web sites add a note at the bottom of all their email correspondence—an *email signature*—listing their Web site address.

(1) In **Outlook Express** (Internet Explorer 4's email program), type an announcement message.

(2) Put the URL on a line by itself to help it stand out.

(3) Address the message to multiple recipients by typing all the email addresses in the **To:** line, separating them with semicolons (**;**).

(4) Enter a meaningful, enticing **Subject** line.

PART 9

Super-Editing: HTML

You've been creating HTML files all along. That's what FrontPage Express creates behind the scenes. That's what all Web authoring programs create.

The HTML file itself is just an ordinary text file that uses the filename extension .htm or .html. Inside the file, you'll find all of the text of your page and its title, plus an array of little codes called **tags**. The tags are what makes HTML work. When a browser opens an HTML file, it reads and obeys the tags, which tell the browser what each object is (a heading, a paragraph, a link), the filenames and positions of any pictures, the URLs to which the links point, and so on.

Actually, Web authoring programs are so good these days that you could really continue to grow as a Web author and never touch raw HTML. But in the course of even an Easy introduction to Web authoring, it's important to explore the easy basics of HTML.

Tasks

Task 1: What Is HTML, Exactly?

A great way to begin discovering **HTML** is to explore the **HTML** file of a Web page whose contents and formatting you already know. That way, you can often guess on sight what many of the tags are doing, which will quickly enlighten you on how HTML tags do their thing.

Click

✔ In its HTML view, FrontPage Express color-codes the HTML tags to help authors see them. But the color-coding doesn't really mean anything, and when you create your own HTML tags, you certainly don't have to worry what color they are!

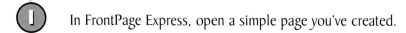

In FrontPage Express, open a simple page you've created.

Click **View**, and then choose **HTML** to see the raw HTML code of the page.

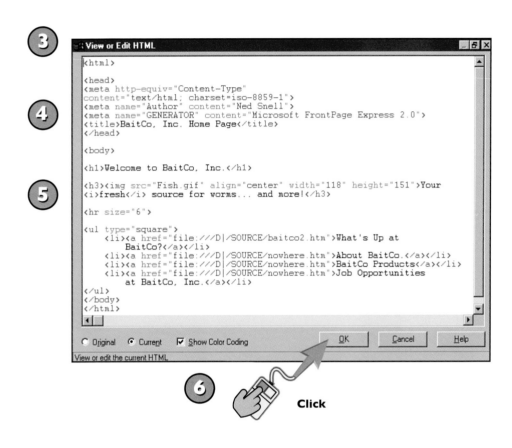

(3)

View or Edit HTML

```
<html>

<head>
<meta http-equiv="Content-Type"
content="text/html; charset=iso-8859-1">
<meta name="Author" content="Ned Snell">
<meta name="GENERATOR" content="Microsoft FrontPage Express 2.0">
<title>BaitCo, Inc. Home Page</title>
</head>

<body>

<h1>Welcome to BaitCo, Inc.</h1>

<h3><img src="Fish.gif" align="center" width="118" height="151">Your
<i>fresh</i> source for worms... and more!</h3>

<hr size="6">

<ul type="square">
    <li><a href="file:///D|/SOURCE/baitco2.htm">What's Up at
       BaitCo?</a></li>
    <li><a href="file:///D|/SOURCE/nowhere.htm">About BaitCo.</a></li>
    <li><a href="file:///D|/SOURCE/nowhere.htm">BaitCo Products</a></li>
    <li><a href="file:///D|/SOURCE/nowhere.htm">Job Opportunities
       at BaitCo, Inc.</a></li>
</ul>
</body>
</html>
```

○ Original ● Current ☑ Show Color Coding   OK   Cancel   Help

View or edit the current HTML

(6) Click

(3) Examine the page, ignoring the tags and looking for the content you put there: your words, the filenames of pictures, the URLs of your links.

(4) Now look at all the HTML tags, which are enclosed in carats (< >).

(5) Observe that you can tell on sight what some tags do. For example, before text to which you've applied a level-I Heading paragraph style, you'll see the tag <h1>—Heading I.

(6) Click **OK** to return to the regular FrontPage Express view.

✓ **If you look closely at the tags, you'll notice that most (but not all) work in pairs. For example, somewhere near the top of the file, you'll see the tag <title>, followed by your page's title, followed by another tag, </title>. That's how tags usually work; one tag marks the start of something, and another tag (the same tag with the added slash at the front) marks the end.**

End Task

Task 2: Creating a Web Page in HTML

Most of the job of creating a Web page in HTML involves typing tags and content. But first you need to understand the big picture, the way an HTML file must be organized into two sections: the *header* (which contains the page title, and sometimes other, optional stuff), and the *body* (the part of the file where you define everything you see in the page layout). Because an HTML file is just a text file, you can create it in any text editor, such as Windows's Notepad.

Start Here

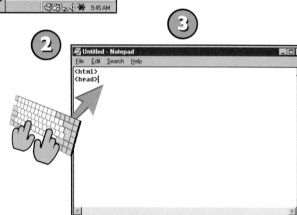

Click

(✓) When you type HTML tags, it doesn't matter whether you use uppercase letters (<H1>) or lowercase letters (<h1>). Some pros recommend using capital letters, because doing so makes it easier to see tags sprinkled within the text of the page. But you can do whatever you like.

① Click **Start**, **Programs**, **Accessories**, and then **Notepad**.

② Type **<html>** to mark the start of the file, and press **Enter** to start a new line.

③ Type **<head>** to start the header, and then press **Enter**.

Next Step

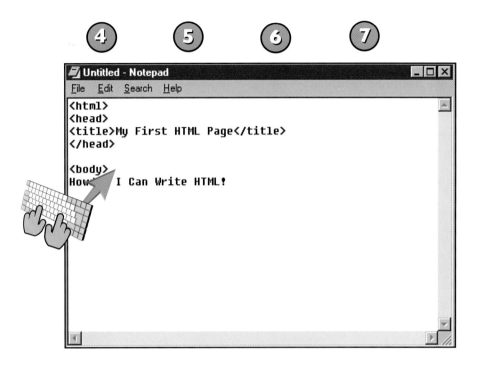

Untitled - Notepad

File Edit Search Help

```
<html>
<head>
<title>My First HTML Page</title>
</head>

<body>
Howdy! I Can Write HTML!
```

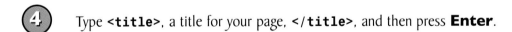

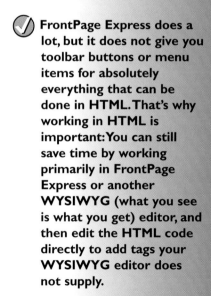
④ Type **<title>**, a title for your page, **</title>**, and then press **Enter**.

⑤ Type **</head>** to mark the end of the header, and then press **Enter**.

⑥ Type **<body>** to mark the start of the body, and then press **Enter**.

⑦ Type **Howdy! I Can Write HTML!**, and then press **Enter**.

Next Step

Task 2: Continued

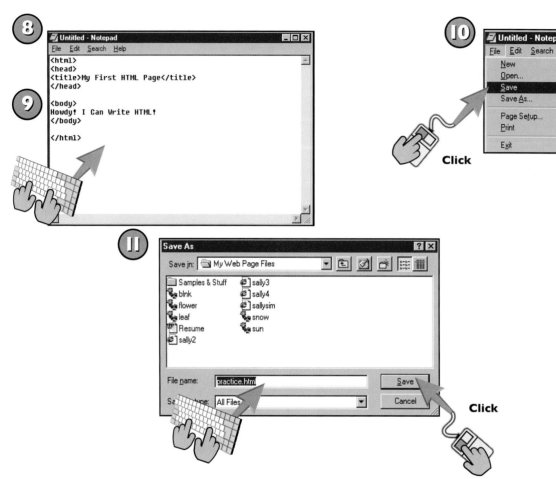

8 Type **</body>** to mark the end of the body.

9 Type **</html>** to mark the end of the file.

10 Click **File, Save.**

11 Choose a folder (or the desktop) in which to store the file, type **practice.html** for a filename, and then click the **Save** button.

Next Step

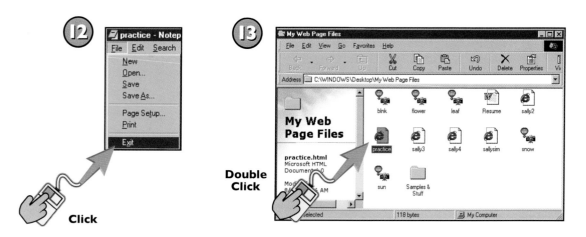

Click

Double Click

If you don't see what you expect to see when you view the file through a browser, it's usually because of a minor **HTML** coding error. If you forget to create both a header and body, or forget to use close tags (the ones with the slash in them, such as </body>), or misspell a tag, the browser cannot display the file correctly. Go back and check your tags carefully.

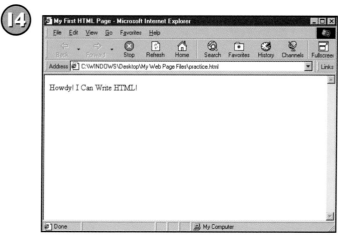

When you choose **File, Open** in Notepad to re-open an HTML file you're working on, you won't see the HTML file in Notepad's Open dialog box, even after you navigate to the right folder. At first, that box shows only files ending in .txt. Open the list at the bottom of the Open dialog box, and choose **All files (*.*).** Then your HTML file will appear in the box so you can open it.

(12) Click **File**, **Exit**.

(13) In Windows, open the folder where you stored practice.html.

(14) Double-click the icon, to display the file in your default browser.

Task 3: Adding a Picture Through HTML

Once you have the header and body set up, you can begin adding tags and content. To get a taste of how tags can work, add a picture to your basic HTML file. Just for fun, use FrontPage Express's built-in HTML source editor to add the tag.

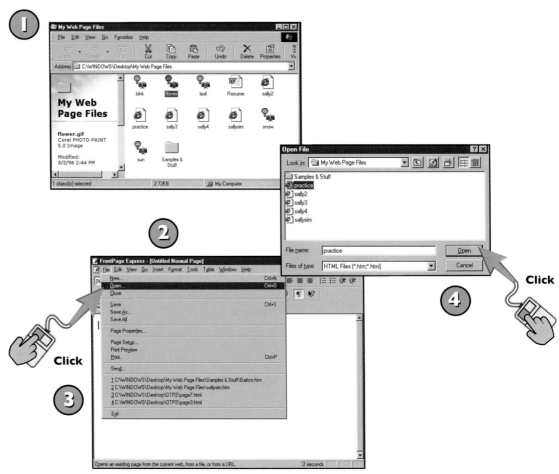

Click

Click

Click

To play with HTML, you can open this HTML view, make changes to the HTML codes or anything else on the page, and then click **OK** to return to FrontPage Express and see the results of your changes in FrontPage Express's regular, "browser" view of the file.

Prepare an image file, and store it in the same folder as the `practice.html` file you created in Task 2.

Open FrontPage Express.

Click **File**, **Open**.

Click **Browse**, navigate to the folder (or desktop) where practice.html is stored, click **practice.html**, and click **Open**.

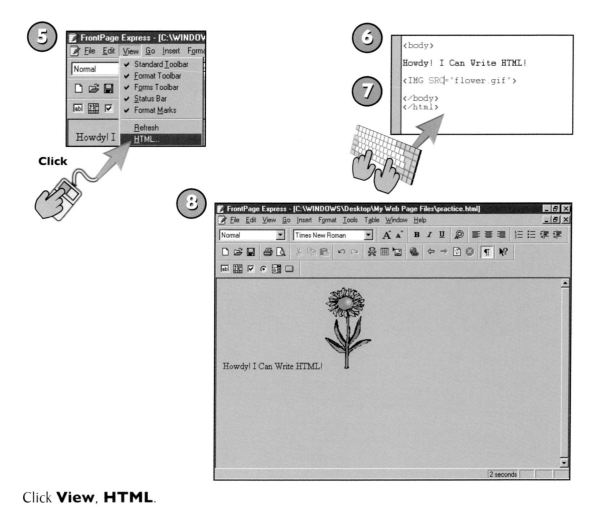

Click

When you create a file in Notepad or another text editor and then view its source through FrontPage Express, you'll notice tags you never wrote, and other minor changes. FrontPage automatically "cleans up" the HTML coding of any file you open by adding some optional tags and by deleting unnecessary (but harmless) line breaks.

If when you view the page back in FrontPage Express view, you don't like the results of the last HTML change you made, you can undo it by clicking **Edit** and choosing **Undo**.

5 Click **View**, **HTML**.

6 In the body, between your line of text and the closing body tag, type **<IMG SRC=** (the start of the HTML tag that inserts an image in a page).

7 Follow the equals sign (=) with a quotation mark (") the filename of the image file, another quotation mark, and a close carat (>).

8 Click **OK** to close the HTML editor and see the changed page in FrontPage Express.

End Task

Task 4: Applying Formatting to Text

The tag that adds images is a little unusual, in that it doesn't work in pairs like most tags. To get a better sense of how tags usually work, add tags to apply level-1 Heading format, center that heading on the page, and make a word within it italic.

✓ Look at the way the `<align>` tag goes inside the `<h1>` tag. Some special tags, called *attributes*, go inside other tags to modify the formatting applied by the main tag. The align attributes—center, left, right—go inside the tags for a paragraph (`<p>`), heading (`<h1>`, `<h2>`...) and image (`<img src...`) to align those objects.

✓ If you want to add more paragraphs to your sample file, simply pressing Enter to start a new line doesn't do the job. You must start each new paragraph with either one of the heading tags (`<h1>`, `<h2>`, and so on) or with a "new paragraph" tag (`<p>`) so that the browser knows to break the line and start a new one.

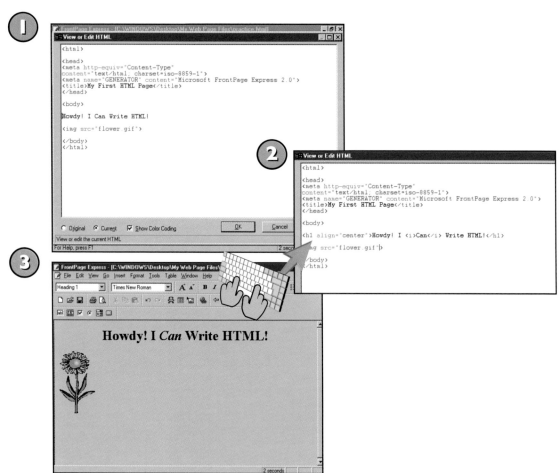

In FrontPage Express or Notepad, open the practice HTML file you created in Task 2.

Add the tags to apply header 1 formatting (**<h1>**, **</h1>**), center the paragraph (**align=center...**) and italics (**<i>**, **</i>**).

View the page in your browser or in FrontPage's regular view to see the results.

Task 5: Learning How to Use All the HTML Tags

Start Here

1

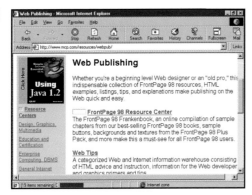

If you want to learn more about **HTML**, there are lots of good ways to get started. Not surprisingly, many of the best beginner's **HTML** primers and reference guides can be found online. Here's a place to start: *The 24-Hour HTML Café.*

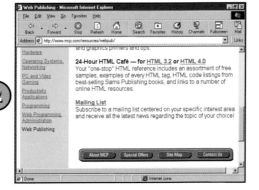

2

3

1 Connect to the Internet, and surf to the Macmillan Computer Publishing resources page for Web Publishing, at **www.mcp.com/resources/webpub/**.

2 Scroll down to the link for **24-Hour HTML Café**.

3 Click the link to **HTML 3.2**.

Dozens of books can tell you how to use all the **HTML** tags properly. The creator of the **HTML** Café, Dick Oliver, wrote *Sams Teach Yourself HTML in 24 Hours*, which is a good choice for an author newly graduated from *Easy Web Page Publishing*.

End Task

Discovering Other Web Authoring Tools and Techniques

With nothing more than FrontPage Express and the occasional bit of HTML editing, you can do 90 percent of the things 90 percent of Web authors ever do.

But before you leave this *Easy* book, it's important to know that there are other tools and utilities you can add to your Web authoring arsenal, now that you've developed a solid foundation through the tools you already know.

In particular, there are other general-purpose Web authoring programs that can serve you when you have special needs, or when you're ready to move up to pro-level tools. You meet a few such options in this final Part, and also learn how to find online not only other programs, but resources for expanding your Web-publishing prowess.

Tasks

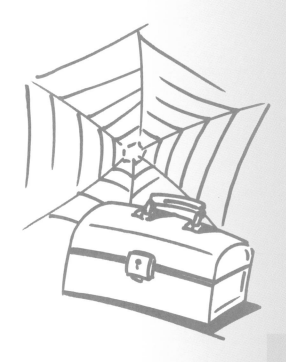

Task 1: Finding Authoring Programs on the Web

There are so many Web authoring tools, including commercial, shareware, and freeware programs. And new tools appear all the time. So being aware of the best-known tools (as you will be, after the next few tasks) isn't enough. To keep up with what's new and where to get it, you need to know how to search for the Web authoring tools available online. Here's a few ways to start.

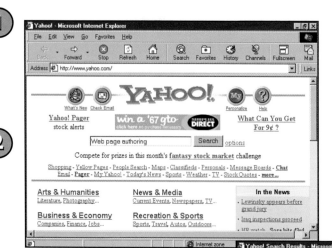

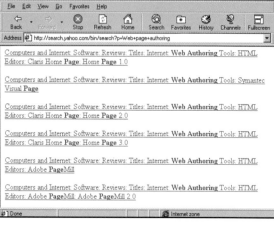

 Other good search terms to try in step 2 include `HTML editor`, `HTML authoring`, **and** `Web publishing`.

 When searching, pay particular attention to lesser-known, little tools, especially shareware products. Often these are more innovative than the popular tools you hear the most about.

1 Go to the **Yahoo** search page at `www.yahoo.com`.

2 In the Search box, type `Web page authoring`, and then click **Search**.

3 The search results will show many categories and sites you can browse to find authoring programs and other Web authoring stuff.

Next Step

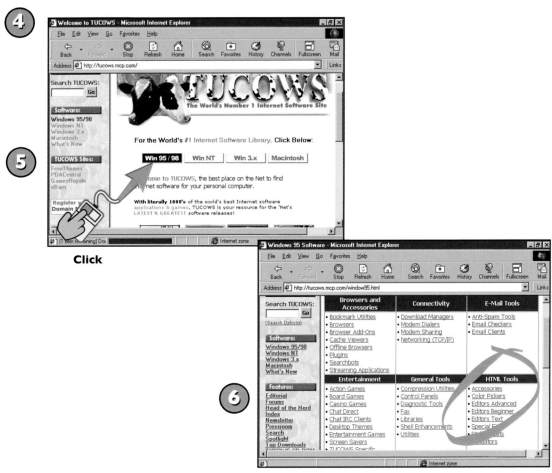

Click

In the **HTML Tools** box on Tucows, notice the link for **Special FX**. This link leads to fun and funky tools for adding animation, sound, and other pizzazz to your pages.

You can also find plenty of tools by visiting the Tucows library at **tucows.mcp.com**.

Click the button for your system: **Win 95/98** or **Win NT**.

Note the links in Tucows' far-left column. The What's New link offers a quick way to check for any new and exciting tools.

Look in the **HTML Tools** box for likely links, such as **Editors Beginner**, and click.

Task 2: Learning About Microsoft FrontPage

On the one hand, Microsoft's FrontPage—the pro-level big brother to FrontPage Express—is the logical next step up for someone who's already experienced with the junior "Express" version. Although FrontPage offers you many powerful capabilities not included in Express, nearly everything you now know how to do is done the same way in FrontPage—so it's an easy move up. On the other hand, FrontPage isn't free. While trying to decide on your next move, visit the FrontPage Web site to learn more.

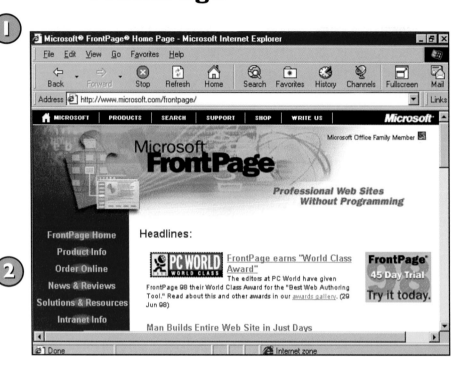

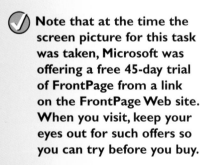
Note that at the time the screen picture for this task was taken, Microsoft was offering a free 45-day trial of FrontPage from a link on the FrontPage Web site. When you visit, keep your eyes out for such offers so you can try before you buy.

Connect to the Internet, and point your browser to **www.microsoft.com/frontpage/**.

Explore the links to learn more about FrontPage and how to get it.

Task 3: Learning About Netscape Composer

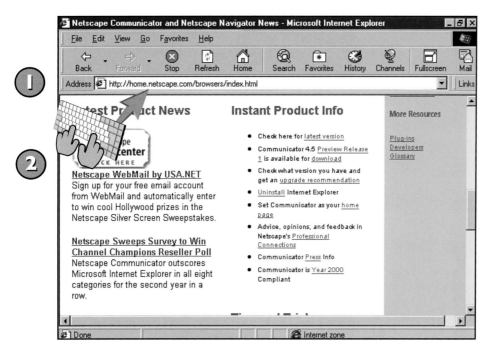

Just as FrontPage Express comes free with Internet Explorer 4, Composer—Netscape's Web authoring program—comes free with Communicator, Netscape's all-in-one Internet software package. Composer is very similar to FrontPage Express, but it does a few things Express doesn't; for example, it gives you better control of the positioning of pictures on a page. Those capabilities make Composer a nice companion to FrontPage Express.

(✓) The book *Sams Teach Yourself to Create a Web Page in 24 Hours*, 2nd Edition is not only a good next book for someone who started with *Easy Web Pages*, but also one that shows in detail how to use Composer. The book includes Communicator (with Composer, of course) and other Web authoring tools on its free CD-ROM.

(1) Point your browser to **home.netscape.com/browsers/**.

(2) Explore the links to learn more about Communicator and Composer.

Task 4: Finding Graphics Utilities & Other Helpful Programs

Elsewhere in this book, you've already discovered several good online sources for programs, including Tucows (`tucows.mcp.com`). But Tucows alone doesn't offer the incredible range of programs and files available from `Download.com`—your first stop when you want to find and download graphics utilities and other useful Web-authoring accessories.

✅ `Download.com` and similar sites (like `Shareware.com`) are great for finding smaller, accessory-type tools—such as graphics utilities—but not for big tools, such as your primary Web authoring program. For those, it's better to go to the tool's own home page (or use Yahoo! or another search tool to locate the home page), to get more detailed information about the program than `Download.com` supplies.

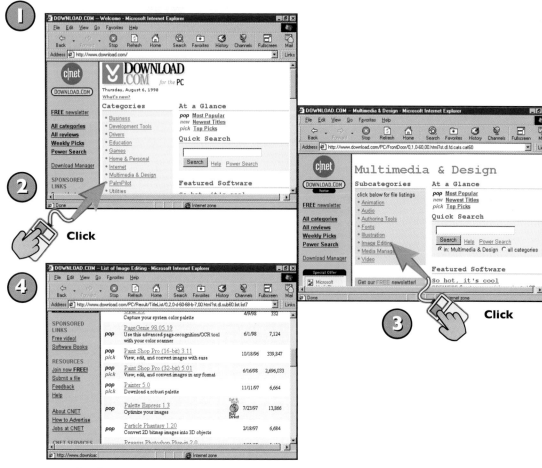

Start Here

Click

Click

1. Go to Download.com at **www.download.com**.

2. Click the **Multimedia & Design** category.

3. Click **Image Editing**.

4. Scroll through the list of Image Editing programs and files, and click one that looks interesting.

Next Step

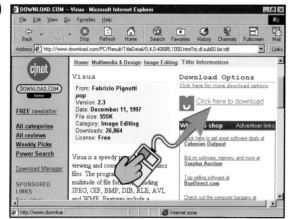

Click

Click

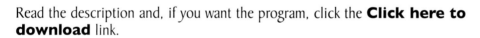

Read the description and, if you want the program, click the **Click here to download** link.

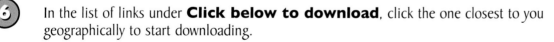

In the list of links under **Click below to download**, click the one closest to you geographically to start downloading.

If you're not experienced with downloading and installing programs from the Web, see the next Task for an easy primer.

If you've downloaded and installed programs from the Web before, you don't need this task. But since this book has shown a variety of great places to download programs, clip art, and more, it's only fair to cover the basics of downloading—to make sure you can get whatever you need.

Task 5: Downloading Programs from the Web

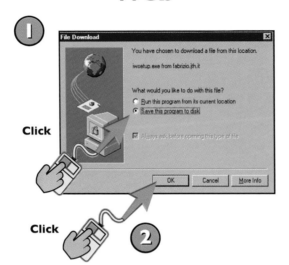

Click

Click

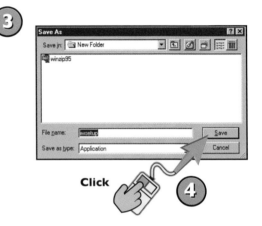

Click

✓ Often, files and programs you download from the Web are *zipped*, compressed into a special archive file so they take up less space (and download faster). A zipped file uses the filename extension .zip, and its icon looks like a clamp around a file cabinet. Before you can use the contents of a zipped file, you must decompress it—*unzip* it—with a program such as WinZip.

Go online, navigate to the link for downloading the file, and click it to start the download.

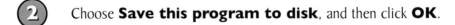
Choose **Save this program to disk**, and then click **OK**.

③ Use the **Save in** list to choose the folder in which to save the downloaded file. (Don't change the filename.)

④ Click **Save**. The download begins. When the download is finished, a message appears to tell you so.

Task 6: Downloading WinZip

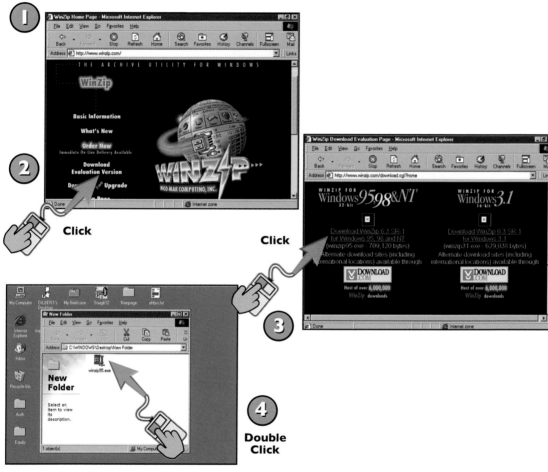

Click

Click

Double Click

A shareware program, WinZip is just one of several programs available online for unzipping zip files. You'll know you've downloaded a zipped file when the file's extension is `.zip` and its icon looks like a file cabinet caught in a clamp. Once you have WinZip, you'll be equipped to take advantage of most of the bigger (and better) Windows programs and file collections available online.

✓ Once WinZip is installed on your PC, you can unzip any zipped file by double-clicking the file's icon, which opens the file in WinZip. In WinZip, you click the **Extract** button to unzip the open file.

✓ WinZip not only unzips, but also zips. You can use WinZip to zip up multiple files into a single archive file you can send quickly or use to save space wherever you store the file.

1 Go to **www.winzip.com**.

2 Click the link labeled **Download Evaluation Version**.

3 Scroll to the bottom of the page, and click the link for the **Windows 95/98/NT** version to start the download.

4 After the download is complete, double-click the **WinZip** icon to install WinZip.

Task 7: Learning About Advanced Authoring Techniques

Where to now? That's up to you. As a budding Web author, you're ready to begin exploring some not-so-*Easy* authoring techniques, such as Java and JavaScript (used for programming scripts that expand a Web page's capabilities beyond plain HTML), advanced multimedia, and more. Here are some good places to begin your studies.

✓ Probably the best place to start exploring Developer's Edge is by clicking the **Documentation** link in the left column, which leads to a variety of manuals for Web authoring techniques.

✓ For many *Easy* readers, much of the material on Netscape's Developer's Edge site may seem too technical. Still, the site is so thorough that it's an excellent place for anyone to get acquainted with the vocabulary of advanced Web authoring.

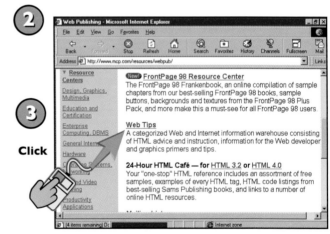

Click

For an extensive selection of tutorials, reference pages, and other advanced authoring resources, visit Netscape's Developer's Edge site at `developer.netscape.com`.

For a more modest, but probably simpler, selection of authoring tips, go to Macmillan Computer Publishing's Web Publishing resources page at `www.mcp.com/resources/webpub`.

Scroll down Macmillan's Web Publishing resources page, and choose **Web Tips**.

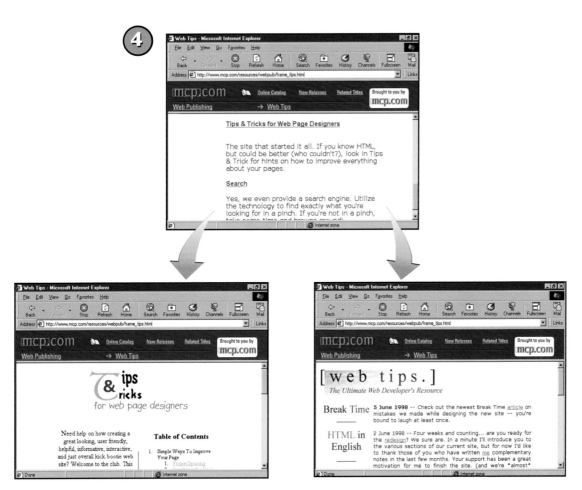

From links on the Web Tips page, you can jump to a variety of helpful sites, including **Tips & Tricks for Web Page Designers**, and another, more informative page called **Web Tips**.

✅ Click **Search** on Macmillan's Web Tips page to open an easy-to-use search engine for zeroing in on information about any specific Web authoring topic.

✅ Observe the links along the left side of Macmillan's Web Tips page. These lead to all sorts of valuable tips, tutorials, and other resources. Explore!

A

alignment   The way text is aligned on a page. Left-aligned text lines up to the left margin, right-aligned text lines up to the right margin, and centered text is centered between the left and right margins.

animated GIF   A special kind of *GIF* image file that plays as a brief animated clip when viewed through a **browser**.

B

background   A color or image that covers the entire area behind the text and pictures of a Web page.

bookmark   An invisible marker in a Web page that provides a spot to which a link can point so that a link can take a visitor straight to a specific spot within a page. Bookmarks are also known as targets or anchors in some Web authoring programs.

browse   To wander around the **World Wide Web** portion of the Internet, viewing Web pages through a **browser**. Also known as *surfing* or cruising.

browser   A program, such as Internet Explorer or Netscape Navigator, that enables you to view Web pages.

bulleted list   A list of items in which each item is preceded by a marker, a bullet, or some other symbol character. See also *numbered list*.

C

CGI (Common Gateway Interface)   One method for creating scripts that make some advanced Web page features work, such as forms. See also *Java*, *JavaScript*.

character formatting   Formatting that changes the style of characters, such as applying fonts, bold, or italic.

check box   A small, square box used to select objects in a program or a Web page. Clicking an empty check box inserts a check mark there, indicating that the object or option next to the check box is selected.

close tag   An HTML *tag* required at the end of a block of code beginning with certain tags. Close tags begin with </.

D

dialog box   A box that pops up in Windows programs to provide the options necessary for completing a particular task. Different tasks display different dialog boxes.

download   The act of copying information *from* a server computer to your computer. See also *upload*.

domain   The address of a computer on the Internet. A user's Internet address is made up of a username and a domain name. Every Web server has its own unique domain, and can play host to other domains as well.

E-F

email address   The Internet address used in an email program to send email to a particular Internet user. The address is typically made up of a username, an @ sign, and a domain name (user@domain).

FAQ file   Short for Frequently Asked Questions file. A computer file, often made available on the Internet, containing the answers to frequently asked questions about a particular topic or Web site.

font   A particular style of text.

form   A part of a Web page where users can type entries or make selections that are then collected and processed.

freeware   Software available to anyone, free of charge (unlike *shareware*, which requires payment), often available for download from the Internet.

FrontPage Express   A Web page authoring program from Microsoft, included in the free Internet Explorer suite of Internet programs (for Windows 95 and NT) and also built in to Windows 98.

FTP   Short for File Transfer Protocol. The basic method for copying a file from one computer to another through the Internet, often used for publishing Web page files by *upload*ing them to a server.

G-H

GIF   A form of computer image file, using the file extension .GIF, commonly used for *inline images* in Web pages.

heading   A short line of text, often set large and bold, that marks the start of a particular section of a document, such as a Web page.

horizontal line   In a Web page, a straight line that divides sections of the page horizontally. Sometimes also known as a horizontal rule.

HTML (Hypertext Markup Language)   The document formatting language used to create Web pages. The files produced by Web authoring programs like *FrontPage Express* are HTML files.

hyperlink   See *link*.

I

inline image An image that appears within the layout of a Web page.

Internet A large, loosely organized internetwork connecting universities, research institutions, governments, businesses, and other organizations so they can exchange messages and share information.

Internet Explorer A *browser* for the World Wide Web, created by Microsoft. Internet Explorer version 4 is built into Windows 98, and available free for other systems (Windows 3.1, 95, and NT; Macintosh; UNIX). Most versions of Internet Explorer 4 include *FrontPage Express*.

intranet An internal corporate network, usually a local area network, that is based on Internet technologies so that using it is just like using a *browser* on the *World Wide Web*.

J-K

Java, JavaScript Two different methods for creating scripts that make some advanced Web page features work, such as *forms*. See also *CGI*.

JPEG A form of image file, using the file extension `.jpg`, commonly used for inline images in Web pages.

L

link Short for hyperlink, an object in a Web page that takes the visitor to another page, downloads a file, or starts some other action.

link source The part of a link that a visitor actually sees in a Web page and clicks to activate the link. (The other part of a link is the *URL*.) A link source can be some text or a picture.

list box
In a *dialog box* or Web page, a small box with a downward-pointing arrow at its right end. Clicking the arrow opens a list of options the user can click to select one to appear in the box.

M

mailto link A link in a Web page that, when clicked by a visitor, opens the visitor's email program and creates a new message pre-addressed to a particular person.

Marquee A line of text that repeatedly scrolls across part of a Web page, used as an attention-getting device.

menu A list of choices on a computer screen. A user selects one choice to perform an action with a software program.

Mosaic A *browser*, available as *freeware*.

N-O

Navigator   Sometimes called *Netscape*, a popular *browser* from Netscape Communications. Navigator is available in a suite, called Netscape Communicator, that also includes programs for Web authoring, email, and other activities.

netiquette   The code of proper conduct (etiquette) on the Internet (the Net).

Netscape   Short for Netscape Communications, a software company that developed and markets *Navigator*. Some people casually refer to Navigator and Communicator as "Netscape."

network   A set of computers interconnected so they can communicate and share information. Connected networks together form an internetwork.

Notepad   A program included with all versions of Windows that allows the user to view, edit, and print plain text files.

numbered list   A list of items in which each item is preceded by a number, and the numbers increase as the list goes down. See also *bulleted list*.

P-Q

paragraph formatting   Text formatting, such as *paragraph styles* or *alignment*, that can be applied only to a whole paragraph or paragraphs, never to only selected characters within a paragraph, like *character formatting*.

paragraph style   The principal form of text formatting on a Web page. Paragraph styles include six levels of *Headings*, a style for Normal text, and several different styles for creating lists.

R-S

search engine   A program that provides a way to search for specific information, such as *Yahoo!*.

selection   Text or a picture the author has highlighted so that the next action the author performs affects only the highlighted text or picture.

server   A computer on a network used to store information and "serve" it to other computers that contact it through the network. A Web server stores Web pages, which it serves to the browsers that contact it through the Internet.

shareware   Software programs that users are permitted to acquire and evaluate for free. Shareware is different from freeware in that if a person likes the shareware program and plans to use it on a regular basis, he or she is expected to send a fee to the programmer.

signature   A block of text on a Web page, usually near the bottom, that identifies the page's author or the *Webmaster*. Signatures often include a *mailto* link to the author's email address.

surfing   Another term for *browsing*.

symbol   A character that's not on the keyboard, such as a copyright symbol. In *FrontPage Express*, you add symbols to your pages from a special *dialog box*.

T

table   A box or grid used to arrange text or pictures in neat rows and columns.

tag   A code in the *HTML* language.

title   The name that identifies a particular Web page. A Web page's title appears in the title bar at the very top of the browser window.

toolbar   A row of icons or buttons in a program, usually near the top of the program's window, that you can click to perform common tasks.

U-V

undo   A feature of *FrontPage Express* and some other programs that enables you to reverse an action you performed.

upload   The act of copying information *to* a server computer from your computer. See also *download*.

URL   Short for Uniform (or Universal) Resource Locator. A method of standardizing the addresses of different types of Internet resources so they can all be accessed easily from within a Web browser.

W-X

Web   See *World Wide Web*.

Webmaster   The person responsible for the management and maintenance of a particular Web page or Web site, sometimes (but not always) the Web page's author.

Web site   A group of individual Web pages linked together into a single, multi-page document. Web site also is sometimes used to describe a whole Web *server* or all pages on a particular *domain*.

WinZIP   A Windows program used to compress files into archives so they can be uploaded or downloaded more quickly and conveniently. Also used to decompress files later to restore them to their original state.

wizard   Automated routines, used throughout Windows, for conveniently performing a step-by-step procedure, such as setting up Windows or configuring it for the Internet.

World Wide Web (WWW or Web) A set of Internet computers and services that provides an easy-to-use system for finding information and moving among resources.

Y-Z

Yahoo! A popular search engine.

FrontPage Express

G

H

pictures

R

S

W-X

Notes